IRISH CATHEDRALS
CHURCHES AND ABBEYS

CAXTON EDITIONS
AN IMPRINT OF CAXTON PUBLISHING GROUP
20 BLOOMSBURY STREET, LONDON WC1 3QA

ISBN 1 84067 416 4

A COPY OF THE CIP DATA IS AVAILABLE FROM THE
BRITISH LIBRARY UPON REQUEST

DESIGNED AND PRODUCED FOR CAXTON EDITIONS
BY POINTING DESIGN CONSULTANCY

REPROGRAPHICS BY GA GRAPHICS
PRINTED BY T.C.P.S.

ACKNOWLEDGMENTS
THE NORTHERN IRISH TOURIST BOARD
BORD FÁILTE – THE IRISH TOURIST BOARD
TONY ROACH OF HERITAGE IMAGES
CLODAGH KINSELLA OF ST PATRICK'S CATHEDRAL, DUBLIN
JOE TRACEY OF MCCORMICK TRACEY MULLARKEY
COPY EDITOR: ÒROSANNA NEGROTTI
DESIGN ASSISTANCE: NAOKO MATSUDA

IRISH CATHEDRALS
CHURCHES AND ABBEYS

EDITED BY BRENDAN O'NEILL

WITH AN INTRODUCTORY ESSAY BY
JAMES STEVENS CURL

CAXTON EDITIONS

CONTENTS

INTRODUCTION

BY JAMES STEVENS CURL

Perceptions of Ireland are often very curious. It seems to be thought of as a small island in mid-Atlantic, and the expression 'out there' is not uncommonly used in connection with the country. Yet the Antrim coast is only twelve miles from Scotland, and, when the weather is reasonably clement, parts of the Antrim and Down coasts are clearly visible from Scotland and the Inner Hebridean islands of Islay and Jura just as parts of Argyll, Ayrshire (including the rock of Ailsa Craig), and Galloway may be seen from County Antrim. Ireland is therefore not remote, and must not be regarded as a small island off the 'Mainland' (a tiresome word often used by ignorant commentators) of Great Britain, for to an Irishman Ireland *is* the Mainland.

Although it has a distinct flavour, Ireland is still a Western European country, and indeed its Gaelic culture looked towards Europe rather than to England (especially after the Break with Rome), even adopting the Gregorian Calendar in the sixteenth century, almost two centuries before Great Britain followed suit in 1752. However, compared with other European countries, ecclesiastical architecture is often startlingly different. There are the famous Round Towers, for example (of which just over thirty are in any way complete), a peculiarly Irish type (although there are round towers elsewhere, they are unlike the tall, Irish examples with their conical caps), and most mediaeval ecclesiastical buildings are much smaller than the mighty cathedrals

Left: Round Tower at Glendalough, Co Wicklow, reconstructed with its original stones.

and abbey-churches of England or France (to name but two other countries). It is worth pointing out that there are not many mediaeval churches standing that are still more or less intact, although the underpopulated countryside is littered with reasonably complete, though ruined, friary-churches and other monastic remains. Contemplation of these buildings quickly demonstrates that fabric of any antiquity is built of stone, and mostly a grey stone at that. The hard, intractable nature of so much building-stone in Ireland resulted in a relatively unadorned and very severe architecture, for Ireland does not possess the wonderful, honey-coloured freestones (especially limestones) of England or France that enabled sculptors and architects to enrich the built fabric of ecclesiastical buildings to an extent unknown in Ireland. Ireland's grey building-stones add to the melancholy character of so much of the Irish landscape, a character undoubtedly enhanced by the rainy climate.

Early Ecclesiastical Buildings

Ireland possesses many primitive small churches scattered through the land, with a preponderance in the Midlands. There are, however, several sites, such as Inismurray (Co Sligo – probably eighth-century) and Nendrum (Co Down – probably ninth- to early-tenth century), where monastic settlements were protected by a surrounding *cashel* or dry-stone wall. At Inismurray there were several dry-stone structures of the bee-hive type, with corbelled stone roofs, and three rectangular buildings, one of which had a stone roof of corbelled construction, and two of which were churches. Nendrum had three rings of defensive structures, several buildings of the bee-hive variety, a round tower, a walled enclosure for burial of the dead, and two rectangular erections, one of which was the church, apparently with a chancel. One of the most beautiful of all early Irish Christian sites is Devenish, Co Fermanagh, where there is not only a round tower, but some evidence of influences from Mediterranean

Classicism in some of the details. The church (known as St Laisren's Oratory) at Devenish may have had a kind of barrel-vaulted ceiling with a stone pitched roof over it simulating overlapping slates or stone slabs by means of ingeniously shaped masonry (at Muiredach's High Cross, Monasterboice, Co Louth, the shingles or slates of roof-coverings are carved in miniature on the crowning shrine – or is it a miniature church?). What is astounding about Devenish is that the side walls are carried forward as *antæ* (a variety of pilaster, but with parallel sides), but these are *antæ* with rudimentary capitals, thus raising questions about the belief that those particular *antæ* are some kind of reference to much earlier timber corner-posts. However, at MacDara's Island, Co Galway, there is a restored church with *antæ* and projecting elements above the *antæ* resembling barge-courses framing the steeply-pitched gables and terminating in winged finials that suggest a continuation of barge-boards, so the timber-framed origins of some building-

types may be recalled in such stone constructions. That does not alter the fact that some of the carving at Devenish is closely allied to Classical prototypes, and therefore poses some kind of influence (however tenuous) from the Graeco-Roman World. Similarly, several doorways in early Irish churches have inclined jambs with lintels over and suggestions of architraves cut into the jamb-stones and lintels (such as Clonamery, Co. Kilkenny), and others (Aghowle, Co Wicklow) have distinct architraves: both trigger mnemonics of Classical origins. Some miniature models of early Irish churches survive in the stone tombs at Banagher and Bovevagh (Co Londonderry) and Clones (Co Monaghan): the last has a representation of the winged finial carved into the solid stone.

Irish round towers are unlike those of Northern Italy or East Anglia, appear to have been erected between the tenth and twelfth centuries, and have doorways and windows varying from simple lintel-covered gaps to semi-circular-headed openings, sometimes of pronounced Romanesque type. All round towers are slightly tapered, some have entasis (a taper that is not straight, but curves gently with height and diminution of diameter), all have conical corbelled stone roofs, and none has a stair (access being by ladder). Timber floors (of which there were four or five) were supported on off-sets in the stonework, and doors were usually well above ground level. At the top of the tower, just under the conical cap, there were usually four openings. If these towers were supposed to be places of refuge, then they were singularly ill-suited for the purpose, for they would act as chimneys if fires were started at the bases, and everything inside would be consumed. They must have been essentially bell towers, and it is likely that the form was suggested by towers seen by travellers to Rome (the towers of Germany spring to mind as possible influences).

The round tower at Devenish is unusual in that it has a frieze of Romanesque ornament all around its top, just under the conical roof, broken by four carved heads. That at Ardmore, Co Waterford, is one of the tallest surviving towers, has a pronounced taper, and also has three string-courses at which the diameter of the tower is diminished. Most round towers are free-standing, but a few were attached to churches: examples include St Finghín's church, Clonmacnois, Co Offaly, and the Collegiate church of Sts Peter and Paul, Kilmallock, Co Limerick.

Inclined jambs are also found at the doorway of the ruined church at Banagher, Co Londonderry, over which is a lintel on the outside and an arch on the inside, a similar arrangement to that at Aghowle, Co Wicklow. At Maghera, Co Londonderry, is a variation on this type, with a remarkably fine Crucifixion carving on the inner side of the door-surround. Window-openings were small, with pronounced splays on the inside to allow more light in, and with mouldings carried all round the interior of the splay where it joined the inside face of the wall, including the semicircular head and the sill

The Round Tower at Devenish, Co Fermanagh.

(such as at Clonmacnois, Co Offaly). Sometimes the semicircular top of a window was cut out of a lintel, and sometimes windows had triangular tops commonly formed by two stones meeting with a vertical joint. With the evolution of architecture, arches were formed over the heads, and splays were pronounced.

Elaborate semicircular-headed Romanesque arches are found in west fronts and in chancel-arches. The finest Romanesque chancel-arch in Ireland is that of Tuam Cathedral: it has five Orders carved in low relief, and probably dates from the end of the twelfth century. However, the most important (and complete) example of Romanesque architecture in Ireland is Cormac's Chapel, Cashel, Co Tipperary, with much blind arcading. As a building, it is unusual for its coherence and completeness, and is vaulted (the ribbed vault over the chancel is probably the earliest erected in Ireland). The influences were most likely English, although there are shades of French and German precedents

11

there too, for at the time of its erection (1127-34) Continental (and especially English) ecclesiastical influences were starting to percolate into Ireland. The north porch of Cormac's Chapel has a pediment-gable (clearly a survivor from earlier, plainer churches with steeply pitched roofs such as that at Devenish) over the Romanesque doorway, and this became widely influential, recurring on many west fronts. Good examples may be found at St Cronan's church, Roscrea, Co Tipperary (where the tympanum of the pediment-gable is embellished with a statue of the Saint), Ardfert, Co Kerry, and Clonfert Cathedral, Co Galway. The last has a pronounced batter (an Irish characteristic from earlier times), seven sumptuous Orders, lovely carving, a blind arcade over the arch, with humanoid heads under each arch, and above the arcade is a triangle of further tiers of triangles, every other one containing a head. But, where the Clonfert doorway (unquestionably the finest Romanesque example in all Ireland) sits in the centre of the west front of the building, the Roscrea example (which has no batter at all) has two smaller, lower Romanesque arches on either side, each with a gabled element over, the whole held between two massive *antæ*. It is difficult to avoid making comparisons with Continental Romanesque fronts where the Classical inspiration is clear.

Architecture after the Anglo-Norman Invasion

The Irish Church, for so long seen as outside the main European ecclesiastical system, began to be assimilated from 1111, when the country was divided into twenty-four dioceses, later increased to thirty-six. In the 1140s, Máel Máedóc (Malachy) Ua Morgair (d. 1148), Archbishop of Armagh, managed to introduce Cistercians at Mellifont and Augustinians to Bangor, and in 1152 Ireland was officially divided into four ecclesiastical *archiepiscopal* provinces (Armagh, Cashel, Dublin, and Tuam) which approximated to the four *secular* provinces of Ulster, Munster, Leinster, and Connacht. From the twelfth century, therefore, large churches were erected, and monastic plans, similar to Cistercian and other complexes in England, began to be found in Ireland. After the Lordship of Ireland was granted to King Henry II (reigned 1154-89) by Pope Hadrian IV (1154-9), Pope Alexander III (1159-81) wrote to the Irish lords advocating fealty to the English King, events that seem to suggest the papacy saw the Anglo-Normans as the force by which the Irish Church could be brought more under the sway of Rome. The Anglo-Norman invasions of the twelfth century did indeed introduce Continental and English ecclesiastical organisation and architecture to Ireland, but it was not a conquest like that of England in 1066, for a century afterwards large tracts of Gaelic Ireland remained relatively untouched. Indeed, Gaelic Ireland began to absorb the Anglo-Normans, who learned Irish, and, to a large extent, 'went native'.

Architecturally, however, things were on a much smaller scale than anything in England or France. When John de Courcy (d. 1219) invaded Ulster in the 1170s, for example, he and his wife established Grey and Inch Abbeys in Co Down, both in the First Pointed style of Gothic, but modest compared with the size of their English models, charming though their ruins and settings undoubtedly are. The Cistercian plan was extremely influential in Ireland, with a tower over the crossing, transeptal chapels, and a southern cloister off which were the chapter-house, refectory, and other buildings: good examples of this type were Jerpoint, Co Kilkenny, and Grey Abbey, Co Down, the ruins of which nevertheless are substantial enough to give us a good idea of what the abbeys looked like. At Grey Abbey there was a spectacular First Pointed west door, with several Orders and much dogtooth ornament. At Jerpoint (which is better preserved) the cloister sculptures are unusual and fascinating, and the battered crossing-tower is a noble composition. Athassel Priory, near Cashel, Co Tipperary, is one of the largest monastic

Grey Abbey, Co Down.

foundations in Ireland, this time Augustinian, and has an impressive crossing-tower. There was also a very large tower (in a similar position to that of St Patrick's Cathedral, Dublin) at the north-west corner of the nave, and a doorway (not unlike the west doorway of Grey Abbey) at the east end of the nave giving access to the space under the crossing-tower.

Several ecclesiastical buildings were constructed of imported English stone (including decorative use of Purbeck marble shafts), and where English stone can be found, so can English design. St Patrick's Cathedral, Dublin, is such a building, and Englishness is clear in its architecture. It was founded as a Collegiate church with secular canons, and deliberately rivalled the Augustinian establishment at Christ Church (which was within the jurisdiction of the City of Dublin, and which was virtually rebuilt by the English architect George Edmund Street [1824-81] in the 1870s). Around 1220 St Patrick's became a

Cathedral, and was completed around 1270. Although much restored (not always with great finesse or scholarship), St Patrick's still *feels* like a mediaeval building in a way in which Christ Church does not, and it is the largest mediaeval church in the whole of Ireland. So in the Irish context it seems huge, compared with tiny little buildings such as those of Devenish, but it is, in English terms, quite small, about the size of Ripon Cathedral in Yorkshire. The interior of the church is vaulted, but none of this is original: the stone vault of the choir dates from the early years of the twentieth century, and the vault of the nave is of plaster on wood, designed to look like stone. These vaults replace originals that fell in the sixteenth century. Minot's Tower, the huge belfry that stands at the north-west corner of the nave, replaces an earlier tower, destroyed by fire in 1362, which had a spire. The existing spire is eighteenth-century in date, and the Lady Chapel was sensitively rebuilt in the 1840s by Richard Cromwell Carpenter (1812-55) in a thirteenth-century style. Indeed, stylistically, St Patrick's is nearest Salisbury, but much less refined.

The nave of Christ Church was begun around 1213, designed by an architect from Worcestershire who appears to have worked on buildings at Droitwich and Overbury. Six bays of his work survive on the north side. The Master of Christ Church (as he is known) employed shafts of Purbeck marble, banded (i.e. joined and attached to the stonework behind by bands of stone) at closer intervals than is usual in England. Also thirteenth-century is the Cathedral at Killaloe, Co Clare, although the crossing-tower was altered at the end of the nineteenth century and given Irish crenellations (a type of battlement in which the upright cop or merlon has an extra cop on top of it). In the south-west corner of the nave is a fine Hiberno-Romanesque doorway, now facing inwards.

On the great rock of Cashel, Co Tipperary, was built (1224-89) the Cathedral for the archdiocese. The building, though Gothic, lacks finesse, and, even though the site is very restricted, its junctions with the earlier round tower and Cormac's Chapel are crude and unsophisticated in the extreme. Although cruciform in plan, with a tower over the crossing (the largest in Ireland, which is vaulted), the church had no aisles, and the chapels to the east of the northern transept were constructed as separate extrusions with pointless spaces between them (other examples of this illogical and wasteful arrangement are found at Baltinglass Abbey, Co Wicklow, and Adare Franciscan Friary, Co Limerick). It should be remembered that Cashel was in Irish hands, and it is clear that any sophistication apparent in Anglo-Norman foundations was lacking in the Gothic work at Cashel. However, the site, on its great rock, helps to make Cashel an unforgettable sight, despite the shortcomings of its Gothic architecture.

Among the mediaeval churches still in use in Ireland should be mentioned the huge

Collegiate church of St Mary, Youghal (with its impressive array of funerary monuments of the great Boyle family, later Earls of Cork), St Colman's Cathedral, Cloyne, and the parish-church of St Multose, Kinsale, all thirteenth-century and all in Co Cork. Yet none of these can lay claim to much in the way of refinement. Perhaps one of the finest mediaeval churches in Ireland is the Cathedral of St Canice, Kilkenny, on a cruciform plan with an aisled nave, transepts, chapels north and south of the chancel, a low fourteenth-century tower over the crossing, and a Victorian chapter-house lying to the east of the south transept and south of the southern chapel attached to the chancel. Unusually, the clerestorey windows (placed over the arches of the nave-arcade rather than over the piers – an eccentricity which often occurs in Ireland) are quatrefoils, picking up the plan of the piers in the nave. An uncommonly rich west doorway is reminiscent of the west door at Wells Cathedral in Somerset, yet another reinforcement of the connections between the West of England and South-East Ireland in the thirteenth century, and there is a lovely fifteenth-century lierne-vault over the crossing. The Cathedral contains several funerary monuments in the mediaeval style, though they date from the sixteenth and seventeenth centuries, yet another demonstration of the time-lag in Taste between England and Ireland, and the building was sensitively restored under Thomas Newenham Deane (1828-99), who designed the timber roofs in 1866. Arguably, the mediaeval fabric and character of St Canice's have survived to a greater extent than any other Irish cathedral.

By around 1300, however, a native Gaelic culture had penetrated the Anglo-Norman colonies, and it should also be remembered that the Anglo-Norman conquest in Ireland had been incomplete, so instability became widespread. In the fifteenth century, for example, Galway adopted the Roman Law of the Holy Roman Empire replacing English Common law, and Galway's

St Canice's Cathedral, Kilkenny, Co Kilkenny.

isolationism may also have encouraged an individualism in mediaeval church architecture that is epitomised in buildings such as the church of St Nicholas, Galway. The rampages of the Scots under Edward Bruce (1315-18), followed by the disaster of the Black Death a generation afterwards, did not encourage much in the way of architecture (and indeed damaged the town-dwelling Anglo-Normans more than the country-dwelling Gaels), although there were, surprisingly, many friaries erected in the first half of the fourteenth century by the Dominicans and Franciscans. From around 1349 until 1539 some 160 mendicant houses, establishments for the 'tertiaries', and sundry nunneries were built. Evidence for the presence of mendicant Orders in Irish towns exists to a far greater extent than in England, partly because Irish towns did not expand very much after the Middle Ages, but in the countryside several roofless but otherwise almost complete friaries survive, making Ireland one of the best countries in which to study the architecture of the mendicant Orders.

Friary towers survive in Kilkenny, Waterford, Drogheda, and Roscrea, among many other places, and the earliest friary-churches were long and narrow, though southern 'preaching-aisles' were invariably added when the friaries assumed a greater evangelical function. A good example of a south 'preaching-aisle' is at the Dominican or Black Abbey in Kilkenny, which boasts an ambitious south window (divided by a variety of intersecting tracery further embellished with pointed trefoils and quatrefoils) almost filling the entire gable-wall. An English influence is undeniable, but then Kilkenny was essentially an Anglo-Norman colony. In the countryside, however, friary architecture was often basic, with little in the way of embellishments or frippery, having a slender battered tower set at the crossing, usually the width of the nave, but very narrow on the north and south elevations. A good example is the ruined friary at Timoleague, Co Cork. Battered walls and towers, indeed, are peculiarly Irish features, and the motif of the batter survived from pre-Norman times. A large and well-preserved fourteenth-century friary can be found at Ross (sometimes called Rosserrilly), north of Galway, at Headford, which, under the protection of the Burke family, was still occupied and in use until the mid-seventeenth century, long after the supposed Dissolution: this was not uncommon in rural Ireland where Gaelic culture survived and English writ was feeble or non-existent. At Ross there is the usual slender tower over the crossing. Irish friaries often had the domestic buildings set on the north side, and cloisters were usually present (though much smaller than those found in the abbeys, because friary naves were about the same length as the chancel, and cloister-size is mostly determined by the length of the nave). Friary cloisters were also rarely of one storey with lean-to roofs: on the contrary, they were set under the friary buildings, except where one ambulatory adjoined the church, in which position it would have been of the lean-to type.

At Quin, Co Clare, the Franciscan friary was designed to fit within the ruined castle of de Clare, and its impressive ruins may be enjoyed today. Between the unaisled nave and the choir or chancel is the usual narrow battered tower, acting as a pronounced division separating the laity from the friars. A large projection south of the nave contained two altars, but it can hardly be described as a transept because it has no relationship with the position of the crossing-tower. Quin friary has a plan very similar to that of Muckross friary, Co Kerry. At Kells-in-Ossory, Co Kilkenny, the Augustinian priory ruins sit within the largest monastic enclosure in Ireland, the whole fortified with walls and towers.

Mention has been made earlier of the fine group of buildings at Jerpoint, Co Kilkenny, where the cloisters were enlivened with carvings of dragons, animals, ecclesiastics,

Muckross Friary, Co Kerry.

and members of the grand Butler family under whose protection the establishment flourished. Another Cistercian abbey which lay within the lands of the Butlers is Holy Cross, Co Tipperary, where the vaulted east end with its huge window of reticulated tracery, illuminates a chancel of great beauty, which includes a very fine prismatory (sedilia and piscina) dating from around 1450, but resembling English work of the previous century, and of rare quality for Ireland. There is also a structure of considerable interest between the two chapels east of the south transept: it may be a tomb or funerary monument, or it may be a reliquary, or perhaps even an Easter Sepulchre. Beautifully sited on the banks of one of Ireland's great rivers, the Suir, the fabric of Holy Cross is largely of fifteenth-century date, and the building was restored under the direction of W. P. Le Clerc. It is one of the finest ecclesiastical ensembles in Ireland, and, on one of the piers at the crossing, is a charming owl carved in flight on the stonework. At Rosserk, Co Mayo, the piscina has a sculptured relief of a round tower on it: miniature buildings in relief may be found in other Irish ecclesiastical buildings, at Northesk, Co Cork for example. Holy Cross has living-quarters above the vaults: this was not unusual in Ireland, for clergy often lived within the church itself, and there are later parallels in church buildings, including the Moravian establishments at Kilwarlin, Co Down, and Ballinderry, Co Antrim.

Mention should also be made of occasional survivals of mediaeval funerary architecture, although Ireland, compared with England, is relatively poor in this respect. Two spectacular examples may be mentioned here, both consisting of altar tombs with 'weepers' (mourning figures) standing within blind arcades, and both set within recesses decorated with extraordinary tracery: one is in Kilconnell, Co Galway, where the arched recess is an ogee and the tracery is of the *Flamboyant* type (i.e. the opening resemble flames); and the other is in the chancel of the priory-church at Dungiven, Co Londonderry, where the openings in the swirling tracery are of the fish-bladder, quatrefoil, and dagger types. Both are fifteenth-century in date, with no trace of English Perpendicular influences.

Ecclesiastical Architecture after the Tudor Conquest

Under King Henry VIII (1509-47) serious attempts were made to bring recalcitrant Ireland to heel, but, despite the Dissolution of religious houses, the change of status of the King of England from Lord to King of Ireland, and the Break with Rome, English writ by no means extended throughout the whole of Ireland, so several friaries continued to survive under the patronage of Gaelic warlords (who were not backward in appointing their own relatives to influential positions as priors, and so on). However, the instability of the country did not encourage the creation of great religious architecture, and the Reformation brought in its wake the destruction of many fittings and artefacts, whilst the Dissolution caused widespread stripping of roofs and much else from religious houses (which explains the astonishing number of ruined abbeys, friaries, nunneries and suchlike, found throughout the land).

After the Nine Years War (1593-1603 – which also saw much destruction) and the subsequent Flight of the Ulster Earls (1607), a serious attempt was made by the Government of King James I and VI (1603-25) to settle the Irish problem by 'planting' or colonising Ulster (then the most Gaelic part of Ireland, relatively untouched until then by English customs, laws, organisation, and language). It should be remembered that the Nine Years War, which clouded the last years of the reign of Queen Elizabeth I (1558-1603), had seen

the landing of a Spanish army in Co Cork (1601), sent to aid the forces of O'Neill and O'Donnell in the North, and there was a possibility that Ireland would be used as a base from which a Counter-Reformation invasion of England would be launched in order to restore Roman Catholicism and overturn the Reformation.

The Plantation of Ulster involved not only private 'Undertakers' but the City of London itself. (A new County was created from the old County of Coleraine to which parts of Counties Antrim, Donegal, and Tyrone were grafted on: it was called Co Londonderry – and it should be noted that never, at any time, was there an Irish county called 'Derry'.) As part of the conditions attached to the grants of land and privileges, the colonists were obliged to adhere to and promote the Anglican Church, and that meant building or re-edifying churches. It will not escape visitors to Ireland that nearly all the mediaeval ecclesiastical buildings still in use (with some exceptions) are in the hands of the Church of Ireland (Anglican), which was, until Disestablishment in 1871, the Established Church in Ireland, and was united with the Church of England.

Where the colonists re-edified or built (often on old sites) churches, they often employed Gothic Survival details, sometimes curiously mingled with un-Gothic features. Some very odd window-tracery (c.1622) survives in the parish-church of St Michael, Donaghmore, Castlecaulfeild, Co Tyrone, for example (rebuilt 1680-5), and it is not unlikely that the colonists sought some reassuring memories of home in the hostile environment in which they found themselves. More spectacular is the Cathedral-church of St Columb, Londonderry, built by The Honourable The Irish Society (the body set up by the City of London to oversee the whole and carry out parts of the Londonderry Plantation) in 1628-33: it is very like an

English parish-church, and its Gothic nave-arcades are refined. The choice of Gothic for the first Anglican cathedral to be built in Ireland was probably deliberate, in order to contrast with the Palladian Classicism favoured by the Court of King Charles I (1625-49) and his Roman Catholic Queen. Furthermore, the City would have drawn upon its own Livery Company of Masons to provide the expertise, and that Company was essentially conservative. The builder was William Parrott (or Parratt), and it is possible that Edmund Kinsman (fl. 1613-38) and Francis Carter (d. 1630) contributed to the design.

The Chichester family (Sir Arthur Chichester [1563-1625] was Lord Deputy [i.e. Viceroy of Ireland] in 1605-15, when the Ulster Plantation began) virtually rebuilt the parish-church of St Nicholas, Carrickfergus, Co Antrim, in 1614: it contains a very handsome funerary monument in the late-Elizabethan style, clearly London work, but the church itself has suffered

Right: The Cathedral-church of St Columb, City of Derry, Co Londonderry.

24

from unfortunate and intrusive 'restoration' in recent years. Some churches were built for use by the Anglican Church, one of the earliest of which was Kilbrogan, Bandon, Co Cork (1614), but rebuilt in the 1840s. Ballinderry Middle Church, Co Antrim (1666-8), was built by Bishop Jeremy Taylor (1613-67), and contains box-pews and a seventeenth-century pulpit, but it has been hamfistedly treated, even to the point of having bull's-eye glass set in the late-Perpendicular windows, presumably to suggest a 'Ye Olde-Worlde' appearance, but only succeeding in confirming the general impression that in Ireland old fabric is simply unloved and misunderstood.

Rather crude Scots Classicism is suggested by the ruins of the church at Derrygonnelly, Co Fermanagh (1623), but the much grander Doric pedimented west front of Rathreagh church, Kilglass, Co Longford (1636), in which was erected the showy tomb of Sir Nathaniel Fox (d. 1634), is of a very different order. In fact, Rathreagh (or Fox Hall church – now ruined) is probably one of the first Irish buildings in which developed Classicism may be detected in a whole ecclesiastical building. Towards the end of the seventeenth century the Cathedral-church of St Carthage, Lismore, Co Waterford, underwent a major rebuilding under the direction of William Robinson (*fl.* 1643-1712), but that charming building today seems to suggest Georgian Gothick of the 1780s more than anything else, and has some handsome funerary monuments within its walls. It is also very prettily sited.

Church Architecture after the Williamite Wars

After the defeat of the Jacobite and French forces in 1691, Ireland slowly entered a century of relative peace and prosperity, and so there was scope for church-building most of it in a Classical manner. A J. Coltsman was probably the designer of the church of St Ann, Shandon, Cork (1722), with its graceful steeple, although the church itself is a rectangular box with a tiny chancel. Coltsman was also responsible for Christ Church (1720), and Cork acquired a further four Anglican churches in the first five decades after the Battle of Aughrim.

John Roberts (1715-95) designed the Anglican Cathedral in Waterford, an impressive structure (1779) much influenced by the work of James Gibbs (1682-1754), and Sir Christopher Wren (1632-1723) in England: its Corinthian columns, set on high pedestals (intended to rise above the many box-pews), carry an elaborate vaulted ceiling, and there were originally galleries (victims of fashionable Ecclesiology in the nineteenth century). The Cathedral also contains an interesting pre-Reformation mediaeval survival in the form of a funerary monument (1469) with admonitory effigy intended to remind us all of the horrors of death. Roberts, unusually, was also responsible for the Roman Catholic Cathedral in the same city, a massive five-aisled structure, again with a Corinthian Order inside.

Michael Priestley (*fl.* mid-eighteenth century) appears to have been the architect of the Classical parish-church at Clondahorkey (Ballymore), near Sheephaven, Co.Donegal (1752), with its Gibbs Surrounds and Palladian east window. Stylistically, the First Presbyterian church at Dunmurry, Co. Antrim (1779), is very similar, although it seems to have been designed by Roger Mulholland (1740-1818), who was not averse to pattern-books, as his use of Gibbs Surrounds makes clear. Mulholland was again the architect of the elliptical Presbyterian church in Rosemary Street, Belfast (1781-3). Also elliptical is the Presbyterian church at Randalstown, Co Antrim (1790), where oculi to light the galleries were added in 1929, when the walls and roof were also raised, apparently to designs by 'Mr Graham of Belfast'. The architect of the original church is not known, although Mulholland has been suggested.

Simplicity and dignity were the hallmarks of many eighteenth-century Nonconformist

The First Presbyterian Church, Belfast.

churches in Ireland, and the general plan of Dunmurry Presbyterian church, with its pulpit in the centre of the long wall at the back, and its two doors, one for each sex, was followed by other denominations and in other places (such as the Moravians at Gracehill, Co Antrim, and the Presbyterian church at Corboy, Co Longford). Curiously, a two-door arrangement also occurs in the Roman Catholic church at Kildoagh, Co Cavan (1796), a simple, low rectangle, with pointed windows (those on the south have the original Gothick glazing-bars, and those on the north have rudimentary tracery). Very basic rectangular buildings with pointed windows can be found at Malin, Co Donegal (Presbyterian), and Templemoyle, Co Donegal (Roman Catholic), to name but two. A very pretty church survives at Ardkeen, Co Down, near Portaferry, a simple rectangle with semicircular-headed windows and Gothick glazing-bars: it is Roman Catholic, but could just as easily be Presbyterian. Often, housing for the clergy was provided as part of the one church-building: examples include St Mel's Cathedral, Longford (Roman Catholic), Castlebar, Co Mayo (Methodist), Taghmon, Co Westmeath (1844 – Roman Catholic), Ballinderry Lower, Co Antrim (1835-6 – Moravian), and Kilwarlin, Co Down (1835 – Moravian). The last has the added attraction of the talismanic battle-garden in the grounds, a topographical mnemonic of the Battle of Thermopylae, intended by its Greek pastor to keep the Turks at bay: it worked, for no Turks came to ravish the tiny Moravian community.

It has to be said that, although there are many churches of several denominations scattered throughout Ireland, not many are of great architectural distinction. Mention will therefore be made of a few that perhaps rise above a lowest common norm. Among them must be included the charming Church of Ireland Classical establishment (1737) at Knockbreda, Co Down (now in Belfast's suburbs): designed by Richard Cassels (*c*.1690-1751), a German immigrant, it has semicircular transepts and a pretty spire atop its west tower. In the churchyard are several remarkable eighteenth-century mausolea reminiscent of the attenuated Classical style of the Adam Brothers. At Moira, Co Down, the church (1723) is again Classical, with a spire on the tower, and at Ballycastle, Co Antrim (mid-century) the parish-church has a Serliana or Palladian window above the door, and there is a spire on the otherwise Classical building.

A curiosity is the Classical cruciform Cathedral at Clogher, Co Tyrone (1744, re-edified in 1818), and bigger than its severe appearance and odd scale might at first suggest. Although simple pointed windows, sometimes with Gothic glazing-bars and sometimes with diagonal lattice glazing-bars, recur, serious Gothic Revival emerged in Ireland with the very fine parish-church of St Malachy, Hillsborough, Co Down (1760-75), with its transepts (over which are towers) and handsome tower and spire at the west end of the aisleless nave. Apart from its architectural quality, its fittings have, to a remarkable extent, survived, including the Gothick *cathedra* (Wills Hill [1718-93], Earl of Hillsborough, its founder, hoped his church would become the cathedral), box-pews, and much else, including eighteenth-century glazing. The architect was probably English, but unfortunately there is no documentary evidence as yet to suggest who this might have been. We know more about the work at Holy Trinity Cathedral, Downpatrick, where the mediaeval ruins were re-roofed and restored, and the building acquired a handsome west tower and enchanting Georgian Gothic fittings in the 1790s, designed by Robert William Furze Brettingham (*c*.1750-1820) and S. Woolley.

Under the aegis of Frederick Augustus Hervey (1730-1803), 4th Earl of Bristol and Bishop of Derry, his diocese acquired several Anglican churches in the late 1700s with handsome towers (some with spires) designed by Michael Shanahan: these simple rectangular churches with their pretty towers (such as Tamlaghtfinlagan parish-church, Ballykelly, Co Londonderry) pre-date a type of building erected in the early years of the nineteenth century with many provided by the Board of First Fruits. Another important patron of architecture was Richard Robinson (1704-84), Archbishop of Armagh from 1765, who took the young Francis Johnston (1760-1829) under his wing, sent him to Dublin to train with Thomas Cooley (*c*.1740-84), and built several churches to designs by Cooley and Johnston (including Ballymakenny, Clonmore, Grange, Kells, and Lisnadill).

Right: Interior of St Malachy, Hillsborough, Co Down.

Perhaps the happiest collaboration between Cooley and Johnston was the Primate's Chapel, Armagh, of 1781-5, an exquisite little building with an Ionic tetrastyle portico and an elegant interior.

Nineteenth-Century Church-Building
Following the Act of Union of 1801 (by which the Churches of England and Ireland were also united), the Board of First Fruits caused many Anglican churches to be built, nearly all beautifully sited, and contributing enormously to the visual attractions of villages, towns, and country. Most are simple halls, pierced with tall, pointed windows, and have small sanctuaries at the east ends. At the west end there is usually a small gallery, and west of that a tower, frequently with superimposed spire. Until 1813 the chief architect to the Board was John Bowden, and soon afterwards each province had its own architect: they were William Farrell (d. 1853 – Armagh); James Pain (1779-1887 – Cashel); John Semple (d. 1880 – Dublin); and Joseph Welland

(1798-1860 – Tuam). Of these, Pain was undoubtedly the most talented, as is demonstrated at the chapel at Cloghjordan, Co Tipperary (*c.*1830), with its handsome steeple set before the body of the church (which stands at right angles behind the tower rather than on axis with it). Tracery is of the Perpendicular type, and the symmetrical elegance of the composition is charming.

Other early-nineteenth-century Board of First Fruits churches include several in Co Londonderry (all simple rectangles with a tower at one end and a small sanctuary at the other [such as Aghanloo]), the parish-church of Buttevant, Co Cork (an elegant building with transepts, and with a slender spire set on the sturdy tower [1826 – by George (1793-1838) and James Pain]), and the exotically free-Gothic parish-church of Monkstown, Co Dublin (*c.*1830 – by John Semple). The Pains also built agreeable Gothic Anglican churches at Mallow and Carrigaline (Co Cork), but were apparently successful in providing competent Classical designs for Roman Catholic churches at Bantry, Dunmanway, Millstreet, and Ovens (all Co Cork), as well as for a convent at Blackrock, Co Dublin.

As far as Roman Catholics were concerned, 'Catholic Emancipation' of 1829 is widely supposed to have triggered a huge outburst of church-building, but in fact the effects of the Roman Catholic Relief Act were more political than architectural, for many quite sumptuous R.C. churches already existed in towns (many dating from as far back as the middle of the eighteenth century), whilst many simpler places of worship (often indistinguishable, at least on the outside, from their Nonconformist equivalents) had functioned as churches for several decades in the country.

However, because ancient sites had fallen under the aegis of the Established Anglican Church, only a handful of Roman Catholic dioceses acquired new Cathedrals anywhere near their pre-Reformation positions: these were Armagh, Derry, Kilkenny, Limerick, Tuam and Waterford. At first, Roman Catholic Cathedrals were stylistically similar to their Anglican contemporaries, and the predominant flavour began to be English Gothic. Good examples are Newry, Co Down (1826), and Dundalk, Co Louth (1837), both in the English Perpendicular style, and both by Thomas Duff (1792-1848). The belfries of both buildings were added to designs by George Ashlin (1837-1921). The Roman Catholic Cathedrals of Ennis, Co. Clare (1831), and Tuam, Co Galway (from 1827) are by Dominic Madden, (*fl*. 1820-31), the latter building drawing heavily on the English Second Pointed (Decorated) style. Thomas Cobden (*fl*. 1815-40) was responsible for the R.C. Cathedral in Carlow (1828). Now all these are in a rather charming late-Hanoverian Gothic style, and indeed Tuam might almost pass as an Anglican church of the period when viewed from the outside. This was before A.W.N. Pugin (1812-52 –

polemicist of the Gothic Revival, architect, author and designer of much of the detail of the Palace of Westminster) and the Ecclesiologists began to demand rigorous scholarship and adherence to one style as the way forward to architectural respectability. As late as 1844 Thomas Jackson (1807-90) designed (1840) the Roman Catholic church of St Malachy, Alfred Street, Belfast, in a sumptuous Tudor Gothic style, complete with plaster fan-vaulting and lavish fittings, but the general layout, with gallery round three sides of the rectangle, and the focus of attention in the centre of the long back wall, is similar to that of a biggish Presbyterian church of the same period.

However, Gothic, and especially English Gothic, was not to everyone's taste, as Ultramontanism was rife, and it suited the agendas of those devoted to papal authority to favour a more Classical style. This may be seen in St Mary's Pro-Cathedral, Dublin, for example, parts of which derive from the design of St-Philippe-du-Roule, Paris (1774-84), where the overall style is Neo-Classical, with a strong dose of Greek Revival. Continental Classicism is the style of another Dublin Roman Catholic church, that of St Audoen (1841-6), designed by Patrick Byrne (d. 1864), who was also responsible for the Franciscan church of 1830 nearby, just off Merchant's Quay.

It is true that two post-Union Dublin Anglican churches were Classical, reflecting a taste for Georgian respectability and London precedents: these were St George's, Hardwicke Place (finished 1812 – where the influence of Gibbs is clear); and St Stephen's (1825 – where Gibbsian design became Grecianised). On occasion, there was some recycling. One of the most curious cases is that of St George's parish-church, Belfast, a simple, dignified late-Georgian galleried preaching-box by John Bowden which replaced the old Gothic Survival Corporation church in 1811-16. Its west façade is the tetrastyle portico and part of the front wall of the Earl-Bishop of

Left: Interior of St Malachy, Alfred Street, Belfast.

35

Derry's remarkable domed elliptical house at Ballyscullion, Co Londonderry (designed, probably, by Michael Shanahan and Francis Sandys [*fl.* 1788-1814]), which was demolished not long after it was begun, and the stone re-used elsewhere. It is certainly a handsome front. The chancel of St George's (1882, designed by Edward Braddell) later acquired its round-arched screen (by Braddell) and Gothic frescoes (by Alexander Gibbs). The church is now known for the beauty of its music and the numinous dignity of its Sung Eucharists. However, most Classical city churches of any quality were erected by the Roman Catholics, who looked to France and especially to Rome for their exemplars. They include St Francis Xavier's, Gardiner Street (by J. G. Keane, begun 1829), St Andrew's, Westland Row (by James Bolger, 1832), and St Nicholas of Myra (by John Leeson, also 1832), all in Dublin. The splendid St Mary's Dominican church, Pope's Quay, Cork (begun 1832), was designed by Kearns Deane (1804-47), a Protestant, the brother of the more famous Sir Thomas Deane (1792-1870 – founder of the dynasty to become Deane & Woodward). With its noble Corinthian interior, elaborate ceiling, and grand portico (added in 1861), it made plain the Ultramontane, even imperial, tendencies in the Roman Church.

There could hardly be a greater contrast (in many ways) between the two Cathedrals in Armagh. The Church of Ireland Cathedral looks to all intents and purposes like a large English parish-church, apart from some nods to Irishness in the crossing-tower. The cruciform building stands on a commanding site where an ancient church had been erected high above the city. Although there are some bits of mediaeval and seventeenth-century fabric embedded in its walls, Armagh Cathedral is essentially a creation of Lewis Nockalls Cottingham (1787-1847), who virtually rebuilt it (1834-7). However, the church does contain some fine funerary monuments, and there is no questioning the historical importance of the site.

St Stephen's, Dublin.

As the prosperity of Roman Catholics grew, so did ambitions to build great churches. The spirit of triumphalism is clear, even though its progress was slightly hindered by the Great Hunger or Famine Years caused by potato blight in 1845-8. Nowhere is that sense of triumphalism, challenge to the then Established Church, and rivalry better expressed than in Armagh, for outside the old city, on a commanding hill, stands the Roman Catholic Cathedral, begun by Thomas Duff in an English Perpendicular style, and already some five metres high when Duff died. After his death, James Joseph McCarthy (1817-82) was appointed to complete the work, but, imbued with the new fanaticism of Ecclesiology and stirred by the thunder of Pugin's writings, he changed the style from that of the early sixteenth century to that of the fourteenth, so we have today the anomaly of a stylistically *earlier* fabric sitting on a stylistically *later* lower part. The tracery is all Second Pointed in style, and the 'west' front (the church is not orientated east-west) with twin towers and spires, looks over towards the correctly orientated Anglican Cathedral. Unfortunately, all the lavish Gothic fittings (screen, altar and so on, by Ashlin & Coleman) have been ripped out following Vatican II and destroyed, and the modern altar and tabernacle sit uneasily (to be charitable) in their context.

How did Pugin's ideas have such success? A.W.N. Pugin's career in Ireland was significant, and began with the chapel of St Peter's College, Wexford (1837). Pugin had converted to Roman Catholicism, and his writings, starting with *Contrasts* (1836), equated morality with architecture, insisting that Gothic, especially Second Pointed Gothic of the fourteenth century, was the only style in which a 'Christian' (i.e. Roman Catholic) country should build. His ideas were eagerly embraced, and led to the beginnings of Ecclesiology, the study of church history, architecture, and liturgy, which had an enormous effect on the Anglican Church too. Pugin's patron was the enormously rich 16th Earl of Shrewsbury who had interests in Co Wexford (he was also Earl of Waterford and Wexford), and so Pugin was helped to gain influence and commissions in Ireland (though he was scathing about the standards of what he termed trashy design which he found in the details in Irish Roman Catholic churches).

Pugin designed two Roman Catholic cathedrals in Ireland at Enniscorthy, Co Wexford (designed 1843), and Killarney, Co Kerry, commenced 1842 (where, unfortunately, the interior designed by the master has been stripped out with disastrous results. Pugin himself remarked that the Hottentots would have treated his work with more sensitivity than did the Irish Roman Catholic bishops). He also designed the theological college at Maynooth, Co Kildare (begun 1847), and carried out works for the 3rd Earl of Dunraven (1812-71 – also a convert to Roman Catholicism) at Adare, Co Limerick, continued after

Pugin's death by P.C. Hardwick (1822-92), who also designed the Roman Catholic Cathedral in Limerick (1856-61). However, after his early death, Pugin's mantle fell on his son, E.W. Pugin (1834-75), who entered into partnership (1860-70) with George Ashlin, and designed the churches of Sts Peter and Paul, Cork (1859-66), the Augustinian church in Dublin (1862-78), and the Roman Catholic Cathedral of Cobh (Queenstown), Co Cork (begun 1867). Magnificently sited above the town and harbour, Cobh Cathedral (completed 1919) presides over the rich diocese of Cloyne, for the building is impressive and lavishly decked out. It also demonstrates an incontestable change of style, for at Cobh the Gothic language is predominantly French, thus making the Continental (as opposed to English) connection plain, and superseding the Ultramontane tendency to favour Classicism.

A.W.N. Pugin's church at Gorey, Co Wexford (1839-42) is unusual in that it draws on Hiberno-Romanesque exemplars as opposed to the more familiar Gothic precedents. Several Irish architects were to turn to Romanesque in the future, but men like McCarthy were to rise on the overwhelming tide of the Gothic Revival. Pugin, however, argued that true English architecture had to be Gothic of the fourteenth century, for only then was English Catholic zeal at its greatest (this is arguable, for it would appear that English religious observance was very significant in the decades immediately before the Break with Rome); McCarthy, on the other hand, saw some connection between the pointed arch, the Gothic style, and Irish Nationalism, a link that, with the best will in the world, is at best tenuous, and at worst pure fantasy. Curiously, when McCarthy ventured into the round-arched styles (such as Thurles Cathedral, Co Tipperary [begun 1865]), he drew not on anything Irish, but on models from Lombardy, Venetia, or Pisa: indeed Thurles owes much to the Duomo in Pisa. At

Monaghan, Co Monaghan, however, McCarthy's design for the Cathedral of the diocese of Clogher (1861-8, with tower added in 1883) is Gothic Revival, predominantly French, and is probably the finest of his four Cathedrals.

Belfast acquired its twin-spired Gothic Roman Catholic Pro-Cathedral of St Peter (1858-66) to designs by Fr Jeremiah Ryan McAuley (1829-73), again very French in style, although the detail is thin and uninspired (as is also the case at the same architect's church of Sts Patrick and Brigid, Ballycastle, Co Antrim [1870-4], which looks much more impressive from afar than close to). Also Gothic is St Eunan's Cathedral, Letterkenny, Co Donegal (begun 1891), which dwarfs the much older Anglican church nearby. It was designed by William Hague (1840-99), and completed by T. F. McNamara (1867-1941). However, Gothic was not employed on every occasion, for, just as McCarthy had drawn on Pisan Romanesque for the Cathedral of Thurles, so the accomplished English architect, George Goldie (1828-87), turned to the *Rundbogenstil* for his Cathedral at Sligo (1867-73) in the diocese of Elphin. Goldie drew on English, French, German, and Irish precedents for his designs, and created a remarkable synthesis of great originality, which ought to be better known. He even carried galleries over the transepts, a few years before John Loughborough Pearson (1817-87) did something similar in his celebrated Gothic church of St Augustine, Kilburn, London (1870-97).

Mention has already been made of the considerable works carried out at the Cathedral-church of St Canice, Kilkenny, Co Kilkenny, under the direction of T. N. Deane in the 1860s for the Church of Ireland. At Kildare, the thirteenth-century Cathedral there was re-edified to designs by George Edmund Street, starting the year after the Disestablishment of the Church of Ireland under the Irish Church Act (32 & 33 Vict., *c.* 42) of 1869 (effective from 1 January 1871). It is curious that, at a time when the Anglican church in Ireland should have been conserving its resources, it spent vast sums on building new churches or re-edifying old ones (including the Cathedrals of Kildare, Christ Church, and St Patrick [the last two in Dublin]). Kildare has no aisles, but is cruciform with a massive tower over the crossing. By around 1720 its chancel, north transept, most of the tower, and a great part of the west wall had fallen or been demolished. If there had ever been chapels to the east, they were also gone. Street's reconstruction is both satisfactory and sensitive (in a way, perhaps, that his work at Christ Church, Dublin, is not), and includes arches spanning between the buttresses below parapet level and set a distance from the wall-face below, suggesting a sort of giant machicolation thereby creating the appearance of a fortified church.

There was undoubtedly an attempt to keep up with the Roman Catholics, whose new and showy churches often dwarfed the

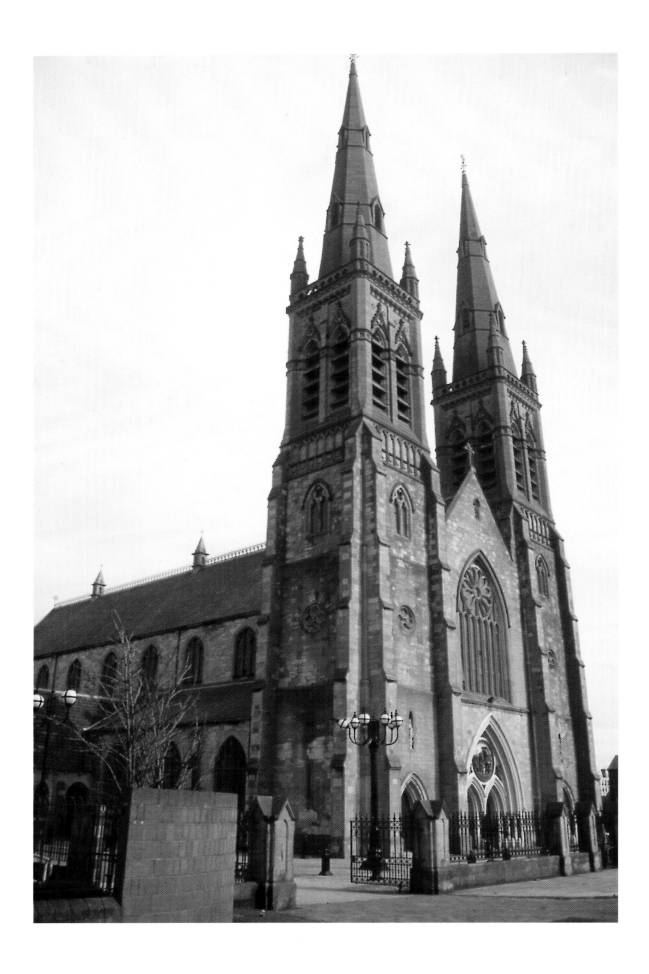

buildings of the Anglicans: this is proved by the almost frenetic building activities of the time. Apart from works on older fabrics, the Church of Ireland built new Cathedrals. The first was Kilmore, Co Cavan (1857-60), designed by William Slater (1819-72), and was quite small, yet incorporated everything a Cathedral should have. Slater also built a twelfth-century Romanesque doorway into the fabric. Deane, in 1861, designed the robust Cathedral of Tuam, Co Galway, to include the earlier (and very fine) Romanesque chancel-arch and chancel. However, of all Anglican architectural statements the grandest was unquestionably the new Cathedral of Finn Barre, Cork, designed by an English genius, William Burges (1827-81). Won in an architectural competition in 1862, Cork Anglican Cathedral is in tough French First Pointed style, with a twin-towered west front and another tower over the crossing: all three towers have spires. If the Church of Ireland had lost its position as the Established State Church, few visiting the building would

think this was so. From its chunky wheel-window over the west door to the marvellously rich apsidal chancel, it is abundantly clear that this is the finest and most magnificent Gothic Revival church in Ireland, worthy of respect for its scholarship, rhetorical power, and superbly satisfying proportions. There is nothing feeble about Cork Anglican Cathedral: it is a building of international importance, and should be appreciated as such.

In the North, Belfast acquired its Cathedral of St Anne, this time to designs (1898) by Sir Thomas Drew (1838-1910), but not finished until 1986. It is in the Romanesque style, and there is no doubt that the earliest parts (the nave, baptistry, and chapel at the west end) are the most successful in architectural terms. The building's transepts and apsidal chancel, though incorporating a gigantic Celtic cross on the exterior of the north transept (*c.*1964, completed 1981, designed by John McGeagh), cry out for a mighty tower over the crossing (Drew's

Left: Roman Catholic Pro-Cathedral of Saint Peter, Belfast.

design included a handsome tower), but are unlikely ever to obtain one.

The Church of Ireland did not confine itself to new and re-edified Cathedrals, however. It carried out a massive programme of new building around the time of Disestablishment, often abandoning earlier and humbler mediaeval, seventeenth-, eighteenth-, and early nineteenth-century churches, as numerous ruins in ancient graveyards (or even in the grounds of new churches) make clear. The work of Welland & Gillespie and Thomas Drew frequently rises to the occasion, and there are often some quite pleasing tracery and handsome steeples to be found. Excellent examples of Anglican churches include Christ Church, Derriaghy, Lisburn, Co Antrim (1871-2 – designed by William Gillespie [d. 1896] of Welland & Gillespie); St Mark's, Dundela, Belfast (1876-91 – by the great English architect William Butterfield [1814-1900] – whose polychrome interiors were often startling); St Patrick's, Coleraine, Co

Londonderry, by Joseph Welland and Sir Thomas Drew (completed 1884); and St Matthew's, Shankhill Road, Belfast (1870-2 – by Welland & Gillespie). Generally, the style used was Gothic, but sometimes Romanesque was employed, as in the enchanting church of St Patrick, Jordanstown, Co Antrim (1865-8), designed by William Henry Lynn (1829-1915) for the Belfast architectural firm of Lanyon, Lynn, and Lanyon. St Patrick's has an apsidal chancel, a rich brick interior, an exterior of masonry, and a round tower with conical cap for the belfry. It is one of the prettiest churches in Ireland. Hiberno-Romanesque was also used for the tiny Anglican church at Saul, Co Down, which is only one cell, but has a short round tower: the building is beautifully sited high on the drumlin landscape between Strangford Lough and Downpatrick. Dating from 1933, it was designed by Henry Seaver (d. 1941).

Romanesque, with varying degrees of Hibernian influence and success, was

Right: Interior St Anne's Cathedral, Belfast.

44

employed by both Roman Catholics and Anglicans. In Kilrea, Co Londonderry, William Barnes (1807-68) designed the Anglican church (1840-3) for the 'capital' of The Mercers' Company estates there, and William Joseph Booth (*c*.1795-1871) designed (1830) the larger church of St John at Moneymore, Co Londonderry (consecrated 1832), for The Drapers' Company of the City of London. However, the style was also used for some Nonconformist churches: two of the most successful examples were University Road Methodist church, Belfast (1863-5), designed by William Joseph Barre (1830-67 – a pupil of Thomas Duff), a polychrome brick building that drew on Italian, and especially Lombardic, exemplars; and Elmwood Presbyterian church, Belfast (1859-72 – now Elmwood Hall), designed by John Corry (*fl.* 1850s), a particularly felicitous essay in the Lombardo-Venetian style, with its *campanile* and main elevation faced in sandstone. Much more powerful, this time French Romanesque Revival, with

a Gothic spire, is St Patrick's Roman Catholic church, Donegall Street, Belfast (1874-7), designed by Timothy Hevey (1845-78) and Mortimer H. Thompson. Inside the church is a fine triptych by Sir John Lavery (1856-1941 – who was baptised in the church). Hevey was also responsible for the Romanesque church of the Sacred Heart, Dunlewy, Co Donegal (1876-7 – which has a round tower as its belfry).

At Rathdaire, Co Leix, the pretty Anglican church (c.1885), designed by James Franklin Fuller (1835-1924), has a west front in which the Romanesque west front of St Cronan's church at Roscrea, Co Tipperary, is quoted, with further ornamentation derived from other Irish sources. The attached tower, however, has nothing Irish about it, and indeed owes more to the Lombardic-influenced *Rundbogenstil*. Fuller also designed the Anglican church at Clane, Co Kildare (1883), in which the precedent of Cormac's

University Road Methodist Church, Belfast.

The former Elmwood Presbyterian Church, Belfast.

Chapel at Cashel is clear. Romanesque was the style chosen for the Holy Cross Passionist Monastery, Belfast, the twin-towered church of which was built as late as 1900-2 to designs by Doolin, Butler, & Donnelly of Dublin. One of the most outstanding Romanesque Revival churches in Ireland is the parish-church of the Good Shepherd, Sion Mills, Co Tyrone (1909), based on Tuscan exemplars by William Frederick Unsworth (1851-1912).

It is very odd that the Irish Romanesque Revival was so sporadic and so late, despite publications and a growing Nationalism. Even McCarthy tended to be mostly a Goth, and one would have thought that the Gothic style, associated as it was with the Anglo-Norman invasion in the twelfth century, would not have found favour among Nationalists in Ireland. It seems that Pugin, the Ecclesiologists, and the architectural press had done their work far too well, and that a tyranny of stylistic taste prevailed. It is even odder, in the quirky history of Ireland, that the Church of Ireland, sundered from the State in 1871, began to seek a new destiny for itself as the true Church, the heir of the pre-Norman Irish Church founded by St Patrick. It should also be remembered that many Rectors tucked away among their books in spacious Rectories, had ample time to consider Irish antiquities, and not a few published scholarly papers on ancient remains. There was also a sense that the Church of Ireland, as the custodian of many of those architectural antiquities, was able to demonstrate a *visible* connection with the past, whereas brash, new, triumphalist, hard, and often architecturally undistinguished Roman Catholic churches could not show any such links. Furthermore, the Roman Catholic Church in Ireland tended to Ultramontanism, so, although its new Gothic tended to be of the French variety, its use of Classicism with an obvious Roman flavour seemed even more appropriate to its agenda.

In a short overview such as this it is not possible to cover everything in detail, but mention should be made of numerous Nonconformist churches, especially in Ulster (where Presbyterianism and Unitarianism were strongest), found throughout the nine counties of the Province. Most are Classical, although sometimes windows were pointed, many had galleries, and often stucco was used to apply architectural detail such as pilasters, mouldings, and so on. On occasion, as at the Non-Subscribing Presbyterian (formerly Unitarian) Greek Revival church at Banbridge, Co Down (1844-6), the architecture rises to excellence, with its correct tetrastyle Ionic portico and dignified Classical galleried interior. Also impressive is May Street Presbyterian church, Belfast (1828-9 – brick with distyle *in antis* Ionic stucco portico, designed by W. Smith), and there are others in various towns, notably Londonderry (Great James Street Presbyterian church of 1835-7 by Stewart Gordon [d. 1860]), Enniskillen (Methodist church, Darling Street [1865-7], designed by W.J. Barre), and elsewhere that have splendid Classical fronts. Ballykelly (1826) and Banagher (1825), Co Londonderry, have Presbyterian churches wholly constructed of Dungiven sandstone, designed by Richard Suter (1797-1883) of London for The Fishmongers' Company Estates. They are pedimented, but have no Orders, and are simple Classical buildings of considerable presence and dignity.

Clough Presbyterian church, Co Down (1837), has Ionic columns *in antis* as part of its temple-front (there is also the remarkably opulent Murland mausoleum in the churchyard, with vast consoles), and Antrim First Presbyterian church (1833-7) has a fragmentary Greek Doric Order of columns and an entablature (flanking the battered Vitruvian entrance-door) set in the plain pedimented main façade. The last was designed by John Millar (1811-76), who was also responsible for several remarkable Presbyterian churches in an advanced,

austerely noble Greek Revival style, but treated with great originality. At Antrim he used the Doric Order from the Temple of Apollo at Delos, published by Stuart and Revett in 1794, and employed the same Order for the most startling of all his works, the prodigious Greek temple standing on its massive podium high above Portaferry, Co Down (1840-1), which would not look out of place in Helsinki or St Petersburg. Millar, a Belfast architect, also designed the powerful but tiny Greek Doric Anglican church at Kircubbin, Co Down, and the Third Presbyterian church in Rosemary Street, Belfast (1831), one of the most grievous losses of the Blitz of 1941. Perhaps even more severe as an example of stripped Neo-Classicism is the Presbyterian Meeting-House at Draperstown, co Londonderry (1843), by William Joseph Booth, an extraordinarily pure preaching-box with pedimented front and *suggestions* of a temple-portico in the simple *antæ* framing panels, but otherwise possessing no architectural fripperies whatsoever.

It is not surprising that Unitarians, Wesleyans, and Presbyterians favoured a Classicism untainted with Gothic in the early years of the nineteenth century. First of all, it was a familiar architectural language, used in domestic architecture and public buildings, and, if applied by means of stucco to rubble walls, was cheap as well as being stylistically very different when compared with Anglican and mediaeval (therefore pre-Reformation) churches. As Nonconformists acquired both status and prosperity following the relaxation of laws favouring Anglicans, so their places of worship became architecturally more dominant, and are often very noble, impressive, and handsome structures, contrasting with the quite humble (but pleasing) buildings of the earlier century (such as Corboy, Co Longford, or Malin, Co Donegal). The arrival of Classicism, with porticoes and Orders (engaged or prostyle), gave the churches of Nonconformity a place in the landscape of town and country. At Donaghadee, Co

Down, the Presbyterian church has an engaged temple-front of the severe unfluted Greek Doric Order: almost opposite (in startling contrast) is the tiny Gothick front of the early-nineteenth century Roman Catholic church. Unfortunately, the interior of the Presbyterian church has been gutted and modernised, and the R. C. church behind the façade no longer exists. Throughout the country many beautiful and historical church interiors, uncelebrated and unsung, have been destroyed in ill-advised and philistine 're-ordering' or 'modernising' schemes, and a huge part of the heritage of Roman Catholics and Protestants alike has been irretrievably lost.

Once Gothic became *de rigueur*, even for Nonconformists, the results were not often very happy. Lavish sculptured detail, aisles with naves, and deep chancels are not suitable for static, congregational tradition or worship, so later Nonconformist Gothic Revival is often uncomfortable and faintly embarrassing compared with the Gothic

Revival churches of the Anglicans and Roman Catholics (though not all of those pass muster either). There are, however, some outstandingly fine Nonconformist churches that are Gothic. Among these may be mentioned the Sinclair Seamen's Presbyterian church, Corporation Square, Belfast (1856-7 – a Lombardo-Venetian essay designed by W. H. Lynn of Lanyon & Lynn, architects); the Crescent church (now Assembly of Christian Brethren, but originally Presbyterian), University Road, Belfast (1885-7), by John Bennie Wilson of Glasgow (1848-1923); and the exquisite Arts-and-Crafts Gothic All Souls Non-Subscribing Presbyterian church, Elmwood Avenue, Belfast (1895-6), by George Walter Planck (d. 1920) of London. Two unusual Nonconformist churches in which Gothic merges with Art Nouveau deserve mention: these are Hillhall Presbyterian church, Co Down, of 1901-2, and Portstewart Presbyterian church, Co Londonderry, of 1904-5. Both were designed by Vincent Craig (1866-1925), brother of Northern Ireland's first Prime Minister, the Rt. Hon. James Craig (1871-1940), 1st Viscount Craigavon.

However, Cork Church of Ireland Cathedral must be regarded as the greatest and most distinguished Gothic Revival church in all Ireland by a huge margin: no other building comes anywhere near it for sureness of touch and brilliance of design. And, taking the wider perspective, it is arguably among the best ecclesiastical buildings in Ireland of any period.

Conclusion

Apart from ill-considered and destructive alterations, the care of ancient fabric in Ireland has also left much to be desired. Crass ribbon-pointing has done immeasurable damage to countless ecclesiastical buildings, while cement-rendering and pebbledash, all too often applied to rubble walls for cosmetic reasons, are among the most dire aesthetic disasters of the land. Many churches erected during

the last century or so fail to rise to the architectural quality of their predecessors, and are often crude and lumpish, with no aesthetic appeal whatsoever.

Padraic Gregory (1886-1962) continued to design in a mixture of Romanesque and Gothic styles: among his more successful works are St Anthony's Roman Catholic church, Woodstock Road, Belfast (1936-9), and St Malachy's Roman Catholic church, Coleraine, Co Londonderry (completed 1937). Some of Gregory's other works are less satisfactory, including the Lourdes Grotto at St Mary's Roman Catholic church, Chapel Lane, Belfast (1953-4), where his use of lined grey cement rendering to simulate ashlar demonstrates his occasional insensitivity in terms of materials (he often used pre-cast stone). He also designed the chapel at St McNissi's College, Garron Tower, Co Antrim.

Very occasionally, there are buildings that stand out for their architectural excellence, including the church of Christ Scientist,

University Avenue, Belfast (1922-37), designed by Clough Williams-Ellis (1883-1978), and St Bridget's Roman Catholic church, Derryvolgie Avenue, Belfast, by Kennedy Fitzgerald Associates (1995). Some Roman Catholic churches, such as those at Creeslough, Co Donegal (1971), designed by William Henry Dunlevy (Liam) McCormick (1916-96 – who designed several other R. C. churches in the region, including St Aengus's, Burt, Co Donegal [1967]), have employed Modernist design.

In the past, buildings tended to be formed from the stones quarried locally, so there was always a sense of churches being anchored to the land in which they stood. In places such as Ulster, where the hard, intractable black basalt does not lend itself to much in the way of architectural refinement, rendering or lime-wash were often applied, and, if architectural pretensions were required, stucco rendering could be employed, notably on the main façade. Churches were also, for the most

Left: Sinclair Seamen's Presbyterian Church, Belfast.

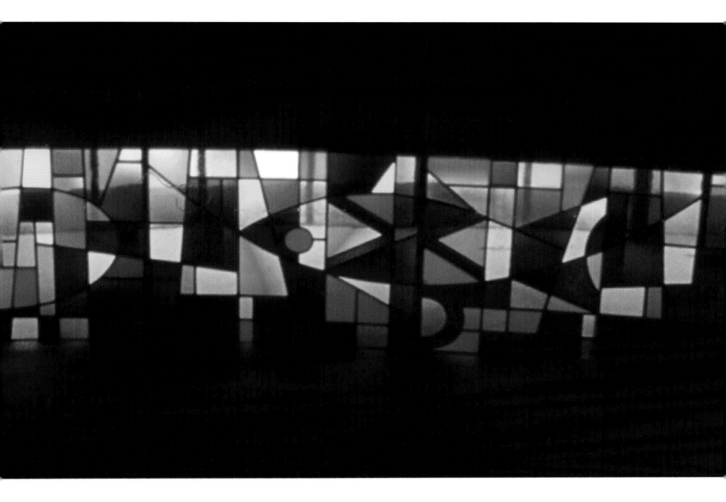

Left: The Church of St Aengus, Burt, Co Donegal, by Messrs Corr & McCormick, 1967. It enjoys a magnificent site overlooking Lough Swilly and the Hills of Donegal. The design of the church was inspired from the circular ancient fort of Grianan of Aileach which crowns the hill above it. The church was declared building of the twentieth century by the Royal Institute of Architects in Ireland.

Above: Stained-glass window from the interior of St Aengus.

part, well-sited, and enhanced their settings. Nowadays, there is no relationship whatsoever between modern buildings and the landscape around, for materials are brought from all over the place, with no regard for the *genius loci*. Instead of elevating the spirits, many modern church buildings depress them, and there is a growing tendency to anonymity and secularisation even in churches. Some church-buildings, indeed, have interiors as uninspiring as a social security office: if they further depress life and its meanings, however elusive, they certainly have added new terrors to death. They will definitely not make evocative, melancholy and resonant ruins, for the Irish climate plays havoc with all man-made artefacts.

James Stevens Curl

Peterhouse, Cambridge,

Holywood, Co Down, and

Radom, Poland,

March-April 2002

The Church of St Aengus, Burt, Co Donegal.

ULSTER

Church of Ireland Cathedral

Armagh, Co Armagh

Armagh is believed to be one of the oldest towns in Ireland. The site of a prehistoric settlement, Armagh is more famous for its association with Saint Patrick, who is said to have established his bishopric there in 444-45, and his church is where the cathedral now stands. There is little left of the original thirteenth-century cathedral as it was extensively restored by the English architect, Lewis Cottingham from 1834-37. It is a plain well-proportioned building in the Perpendicular Gothic style.

Thackeray visiting in 1842, particularly admired the eighteenth-century monuments inside. These include a statue of Sir Thomas Molyneux by Roubiliac, a recumbent statue of Dean Drelincourt by the Flemish sculptor Rysbrack, and a bust of Archbishop Robinson by Nollekens. The north transept contains seventeenth-century memorials to the Earls of Charlemont which are set in the west wall. There is also a collection of pagan stone figures and sculptured fragments from earlier cathedrals. The Royal Irish Fusiliers' chapel is in the south transept.

One of the beautiful features of this cathedral is the eleventh-century Market Cross which is composed of two crosses which are mounted, with one on top of the other. The crosses show scenes from the Old and New Testament. There is also a commemorative plaque, which states that the body of Brian Boru, the High King of

Left: View of the Church of Ireland Cathedral from the Roman Catholic Cathedral, Armagh.

Ireland, who was killed at the Battle of Clontarf, in 1014, lies in the vicinity.

St Patrick's Roman Catholic Cathedral

Armagh, Co Armagh

This most impressively sited cathedral is a fine example of the Gothic Revival. The twin-spired cathedral stands at the head of a flight of 200 steps, linking seven terraces.

Begun in 1840 to designs of Thomas Duff, it was then passed on to J.J. McCarthy, known as the 'Irish Pugin', the most famous of the neo-Gothic Irish architects. He also designed Roman Catholic cathedrals in Derry, Monaghan, and Thurles and the tower at Ennis. McCarthy changed Duff's original architectural style from Perpendicular to the earlier Decorated, which was in ecclesiological circles considered the acme of mediaeval Gothic. Duff had proposed three towers but this was changed in favour of two west towers surmounted by spires with lucarnes sixty-four metres high. Built of local limestone quarried close to Naven Point, the nave was made using piers and arcades, and Bath stone for the groining of the aisles.

The cathedral was consecrated on 27 July 1904, and the new Archbishop, Michael Logue (1887-1924), travelled widely across the European Continent. Having viewed a host of beautifully decorated churches, he was inspired to have the interior of Armagh Cathedral richly decorated. The work was begun to designs by Ashlin & Coleman in 1900, but all that work was removed following Vatican II (1962-65). Among its decrees was one concerning liturgical re-ordering, calling for the redesigning of sanctuaries to make the clergy more visible to the people. With the principle of greater visibility in mind, the beautiful screens, high altar, and pulpit were removed. Their simple, even stark replacements, made from Wicklow granite, now look strangers in this intricately decorated Gothic Revival church.

Right: St Patrick's Roman Catholic Cathedral.

Saul Church, Strangford, Co Down.

Saul Church

Strangford, Co Down

Erected in 1932 by the Church of Ireland, in a Hiberno-Romanesque revival style, this church is on the site of an important twelfth-century monastery, where St Patrick's abbey is thought to have been. It was built to commemorate the fifteenth centenary of the saint's landfall, and contains a thirteenth-century font basin and a small, informative permanent exhibition. In the churchyard is an early Christian mortuary house.

Ardtole Church

Down, Co Down

A fifteenth-century church dedicated to St Nicholas, with a door in the north and south walls, but spoliation down the centuries has robbed its openings of any decorative stonework. However, a cross-decorated slab of the Early Christian period, now in the Roman Catholic church at Chapeltown, just over a mile to the north-east, was removed from Ardtole in 1791, showing that the site has a longer tradition than the surviving church would suggest.

Devenish

Devenish Island, Co Fermanagh

The wooded surroundings of Lower Lough Erne provide the setting of one of Ulster's best preserved ancient monastries. It was founded by St Molaise of Devenish in the sixth century.

The principle building surviving is the particularly fine, twelfth-century Round Tower with Romanesque decoration below the conical cap. There is also an intricately carved fifteenth-century high cross in the graveyard.

Enniskillen Cathedral

Enniskillen, Co Fermanagh

The Cathedral Church of St Macartin (Church of Ireland) stands on the site of a seventeenth-century church. Originally dedicated to St Anne, mother of the Blessed Virgin, the building was elevated to cathedral status in 1921, more than 200 years after it was built. This was largely due to demographics: the population of Enniskillen rose sharply in the early years of the twentieth century. The cathedral tower survives from the seventeenth-century church, and contains a bell cast from a cannon used in the Battle of the Boyne. Colours of the Inniskilling regiments hang in the light and airy late Georgian interior. Notable features are the seventeenth-century font and a stone tablet to William Pokrich (d. 1628) with half the inscription upside-down.

Clogher Cathedral

Clogher, Co Tyrone

The Cathedral Church of St Macartan (Church of Ireland) preserves what may be the oldest Christian monument on the site – a sundial of c.700-900AD. To the west of the cathedral there are fragments of at least three different High Crosses mounted together to form two separate standing crosses. They date to around the ninth or tenth century. The cathedral lies within a large Celtic hill-fort, probably from the fourth or fifth century. Designed by James Martin and built between 1740-44, the original appearance of the cathedral is unclear today. The architect described it simply as being 'in the English style', but in 1816 much of his design was swept away when the Dean, Richard Bagwell, reordered the cathedral 'in the Grecian style'. What remains unchanged is a sense of loftiness, from the building's hillside position.

Long Tower Church

Derry, Co Londonderry

The first post-Reformation Roman Catholic church was built in 1786, costing £2,800, with support from the liberal Protestant Earl-Bishop. The church was enlarged and rebuilt between 1818 and 1909. The interior is decorated in a manner similar to the German 'Nazarene' movement, which intended to restore the quality of religious art. It is one of the most elaborately decorated churches in Ireland.

St Eugene's Cathedral

Derry, Co Londonderry

This plain Gothic Revival building by J.J. McCarthy, with a nave-arcade. The nave-arcade resembles aspects of St Columb's Catholic Cathedral. Its distinctive tall spire was added in 1903.

First Presbyterian Church

Derry, Co Londonderry

In the early eighteenth century, the architectural choice of Greek Revival was popular for façades of Presbyterian churches. This church has a chaste and handsome front, with a fine portico of four fluted columns. Behind the pulpit are stained-glass windows representing the four evangelists.

St Augustine's Church

Derry, Co Londonderry

Originally the site of an ancient Augustian abbey, this was erected in 1872, replacing the previous 'Chapel of Ease' built by Sir Henry Docwra for the settlers. Sited on the West Wall near Bishop's Gate, this beautiful little Church of Ireland Chapel stands as a fine example of Derry's long and vivid history.

Dungiven Priory

Dungiven, Co Londonderry

The burial place of the O'Cahan chieftain Cooey-na-Gal, most notable for the fourteenth-century figure which adorns it. The deceased is represented lying full-length on a slab, above six trefoil-arched niches containing figures of gallowglass. The canopy has superb curvilinear tracery. The abbey was founded *c*.1100 by the O'Cahans who had their stronghold there, and restored in 1397 by the Archbishop of Armagh. Dungiven Castle stands nearby.

Walter's Church

Newtownards, Co Down

The ruins with a seventeenth-century square tower in Court Square incorporate the nave of Walter's Church. The family vault of the Londonderrys, who succeeded the Montgomerys as landlords of Newtownards, is in a corner.

Ardboe Cross

Cookstown, Co Tyrone

The only surviving remnant of an early monastery here is the ninth- or tenth-century High Cross, situated on a dominant hillock overlooking the lake. It would appear to be the only High Cross in Northern Ireland where the shaft and head of the cross are likely to have belonged together originally (there is some damage to the upper part, however). Nearby, in the graveyard, are the remains of the late mediaeval church and, in a field to the north, is a small, featureless building known as the 'abbey', said to have been the home of St Colman of Dromore (d. 610).

St Columb's Cathedral

London Street, Derry, Co Londonderry

The city of Londonderry was the jewel in the crown of the Ulster Plantations. It was laid out by the City of London in the early seventeenth century according to contemporary principles of town planning, imported from the continent (the original street layout has survived to the present almost intact). More importantly, the city was enclosed by massive stone and earthen fortifications. Derry was the last walled city built in Ireland and the only city on the island whose walls survive almost complete. Among the city's new buildings was St Columb's Cathedral, built 1628-33 by the City of London. This Anglican cathedral is one of the most important seventeenth-century buildings in the country and was the first specifically Protestant cathedral erected in these islands following the Reformation.

Built in 1633, this Anglican Cathedral provides excellent views over the city and the surrounding area. The western tower, which was added in the early nineteenth century, is surmounted by a well-proportioned spire rising to 191 feet and carries a peal of thirteen bells, eight of which date from the seventeenth century. They were recast in 1929 when five more were added. The bells of the St Columb's Cathedral tolled to mark the end of the siege of the city. The fine open-timbered roof is supported by sixteen sculptured stone corbels. The Siege Memorial window, which was given in 1913 by descendants of the City Defenders, and the preserved shell, which was fired into the Cathedral precincts, can be found in the west entry to the Cathedral.

Banagher

Co Londonderry

Banagher is said to have been founded by Muiredagh O'Heney, a saint of unknown date associated with a well-known local family. The church is unlikely to date from before the twelfth century, with inclining jambs in the early Irish tradition, a massive lintel on the exterior doorway and an arch within. In the early thirteenth century, a chancel was added to the east end, and the east wall to the original church was replaced by a chancel arch. To the south-east of the church is a house-shaped gabled 'mortuary house', of the twelfth or early thirteenth century, bearing the figure of a bishop or abbot on the west gable. It seems likely that this represents the founder, whose reliquary tomb this was. It must have acted as a focal point for mediaeval pilgrims who would have come to venerate the O'Heney saint, and sand is still taken from it to protect the members of his family. Beside the gate is the 'residence', a mediaeval two- or three-storey structure which housed the clerics of the place. A rough cross stands to the east of the church, beside the entrance to the church-yard, and outside the wall there is a bullaun stone. The depression in the stone is still clearly visible – from which water would have been taken to cure ailments. To the north-west of the church, close to the road, there is a further rough cross.

Cathedral of the Holy and Undivided Trinity, Downpatrick

Downpatrick, Co Down

The name Downpatrick comprises two elements. The first: 'dun', means an early Irish fortified site (on which the present cathedral was erected). But it is the second element of the name that has led some to speculate that Ireland's national apostle is buried here. There is no early tradition however to substantiate the claim, and the inscribed stone allegedly marking the saint's burial place just south of the cathedral dates from as recently as 1900. Very little is known of the early history of the site until the twelfth century, when a church dedicated to the Holy Trinity is recorded. The Cathedral Church of the Holy and Undivided Trinity (Church of Ireland), was refurbished and restored in 1789-1812, when it acquired its fine Georgian Gothic interior furnishings. It also preserves earlier crosses; there are fragments of two ninth- or tenth-century crosses in the modern tower

vestibule. The baptismal font may be the base of an early cross, and outside the east end of the church two further fragments of a cross were mounted together in 1897. A Round Tower which stood close to the cathedral was demolished for safety reasons almost two centuries ago.

First Presbyterian Church

Banbridge, Co. Down

An excellent example of a nineteenth-century Ulster Presbyterian church built in 1846 in the Greek Revival manner.

Movilla Abbey

Down, Co Down

Movilla was one of the most important monastic foundations in early Christian Ulster. It was founded by St Finnian who died in 579. One of its most famous monks was Marianus Scottus, a scholar and recluse who, after he was banished in 1056, became famous on the Continent. In 1135, St Malachy of Armagh introduced the

Right: Downpatrick Cathedral, Co Down.

Augustinian Canons, and it is their mediaeval church which survives beside the road. Built against the interior north wall is the finest surviving collection of thirteenth-century foliate coffin lids, with swords indicating male burials and scissors a female.

Grey Abbey

Greyabbey, Co Down

The ruins of this Cistercian abbey are sited near Strangford Lough. Founded in 1193 by Affreca, wife of John de Courcy, the chief feature of the ruins is the aisle-less church, a good example of the thirteenth-century Gothic style. With a beautiful west doorway, the three engaged colonnettes on either side are separated by mouldings, from which springs a pointed arch.

Inch Cistercian Abbey

Downpatrick, Co Down

Cistercians were brought from Furness in Lancashire to construct the monastic buildings, which were laid out according to the accustomed Cistercian ground plan.

Left: Downpatrick Cathedral, Co Down.

Only the choir with its graceful triple lancet windows in the east gable survives to anything like its original height. The monastery was a centre of English influence to such an extent that the Irish were debarred in 1380. Twenty-four years later, the abbey was burned and that, perhaps together with the collapse of a central tower and a dwindling community, provided the impetus to reduce the size of the nave by building a new west wall. The monastery had been suppressed by 1541. Lying apart are two separate buildings, an oven in one of them indicating its former use as a bakehouse for the monastery.

The site of Inch Abbey beside the marshy bank of the River Quoile was carefully chosen, as it is within sight of Downpatrick Cathedral and Mound. The location is on the site of a much earlier monastery known as Inis Cumhscraigh, which was surrounded by a large earthwork discovered by means of aerial photography, and which was already in existence by the year 800.

St Malachy's parish-church

Hillsborough, Co Down

This beautiful church is sited on a hillside off the main street, and approached along an avenue of lime trees, interspersed with rhododendrons. Externally, the church has a three-storey tower, capped by pinnacles set at the corners. Dating back to 1636 it was re-edified by Wills Hill, the first Marquess of Downshire, in 1773. It has an excellent Georgian Gothick interior, with a superb pulpit, dark oak box-pews and a curved organ-loft.

Hillsborough takes its name from Sir Arthur Hill, who, in about 1650, built Hillsborough Fort, which with its eight-foot-high earth ramparts and stone revetments, looks over the town.

Right: St Malachy's parish-church Hillsborough, Co Down.

St Anne's Church of Ireland Cathedral

Belfast, Co Antrim

Although the work of eight architects over a period of 80 years, in a Romanesque Revival style, this building is surprisingly harmonious.

It was begun in 1899 from designs of Sir Thomas Drew. The twenty-six-metre-long nave has a floor of maple and Irish marble, and at its west end is a maze. The tomb of Unionist leader Lord Carson (1854-1935) is located here. The capitals of the nave arcade are by Rosamund Praeger and Morris Harding, and represent the Occupations of Mankind, above which are corbels commemorating leaders of the Church of Ireland. Stained-glass windows are by A.K. Nicholson and Patrick Pye.

It has an important cross-community, civic and religious role and is often used for services with a national, international, or non-denominational character.

Left: St Anne's Church of Ireland Cathedral.

Above: St Malachy's Church, Belfast.
Left: St Anne's Church of Ireland Cathedral, Belfast.

St Malachy's Church

Belfast, Co Antrim

This early Gothic Revival church was designed by Thomas Jackson and completed in 1840. The exterior of this Roman Catholic church has slender castellated turrets at the corners and flanking the central gable. The beautiful interior is most impressive with a fan-vaulted ceiling, based on the Henry VII Chapel in Westminster Abbey, complete with icing-sugar pendants.

St Mary's Church, Belfast.

St Mary's Church

Belfast, Co Antrim

St Mary's in Chapel Lane, is the first Roman Catholic church in Belfast and was largely paid for by Protestant subscription in 1783. The Lourdes Grotto of St Mary's adjoining the church was designed by Padraic Gregory and built in 1953-4.

Elmwood Presbyterian Church

Belfast, Co Antrim

Designed by John Corry, this late Lombardo-Venetian former church has an arcaded portico and elegant *campanile*. The interior has a finely executed plaster frieze, which combines in its design running chevrons, Neo-Classical foliage, brattishing, quatre-foils and Baroque consoles. The building is now used as a concert hall (the Elmwood).

First Presbyterian Church

Belfast, Co Antrim

Dating from 1783 and designed by Roger Mulholland, this is one of the most interesting church interiors in Belfast. Both the pews and the graceful galleries are original.

St George's Parish Church

Belfast, Co Antrim

Designed by John Bowden, St George's church (Church of Ireland) was completed in 1816. Its Corinthian portico from the Earl-Bishop of Derry's unfinished palace at Ballyscullion is of particular interest.

St George's Parish Church, Belfast.

St Matthew's Church

Woodvale, Belfast, Co Antrim

Designed on a clover-leaf plan by Welland and Gillespie of Dublin, this Church of Ireland church has been constructed from polychrome brick. An Irish Round Tower in yellow brick rises above the church, and is noteworthy for its elongated conical roof and tall lancet windows. Courses of red brick round the tower, a decoration which also serves to indicate the line of the tread of the winding stair within.

St Patrick's Church

Jordanstown, Co Antrim

Built in a Hiberno-Romanesque style between 1865-8 by William Henry Lynn (1829-1915), this is one of the prettiest churches in all Ireland. The church has an apsidal chancel, a rich brick interior, an exterior of masonry, and a round tower with a conical cap for the belfry.

The Cathedral Church

of St Peter

Belfast, Co Antrim

This Gothic Revival cathedral (Roman Catholic) is the work of two architects. Plans were originally drawn up by Father Jeremiah Ryan McAuley, a Belfast priest who had qualified and practised as an architect before ordination in 1858. After construction began in 1860, McAuley left Belfast for the Irish College in Salamanca in Spain, and he was succeeded by John

Far right: The Cathedral Church of St Peter, Belfast.
Below right: Details on the west front, Cathedral Church of Saint Peter.

O'Neill, a Belfast architect, under whose supervision the the building was mostly finished by 1866.

St Peter's was built of Scrabo sandstone with Scottish stone dressing. The nave is aisled but without transepts. Although long known as 'the Pro-Cathedral', it was formally dedicated a cathedral church on 29 June 1986.

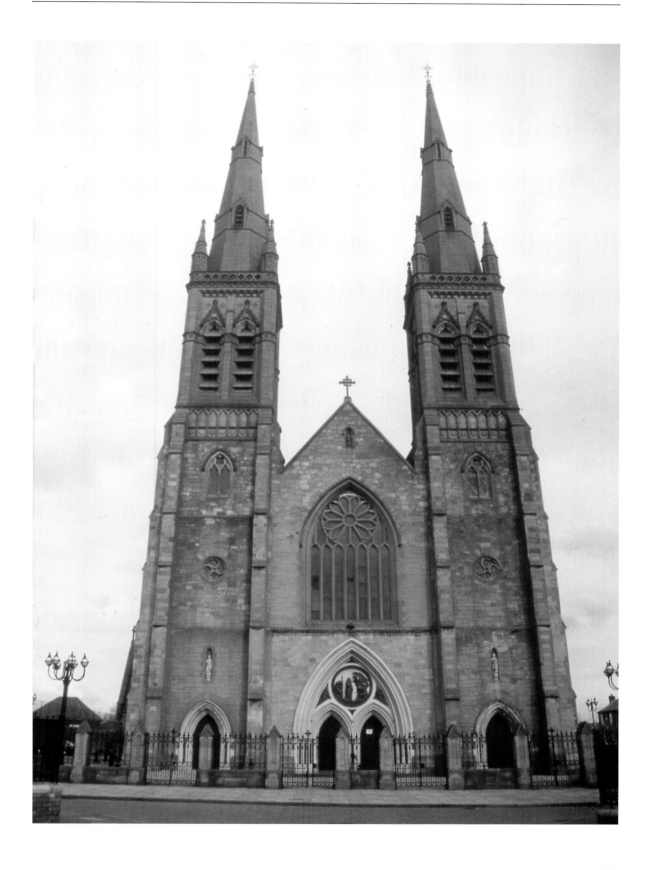

Sinclair Seamen's Church

Belfast, Co Antrim

Completed in 1856 and designed by Lanyon and Lynn, this Presbyterian church is an L-shaped Lombardo-Romanesque building with a tall campanile. It is also part-museum, with the pulpit lectern in the form of a ship's prow, flanked by navigation lights from a Guinness barge. The baptismal font is a converted compass binnacle. This maritime theme is sustained throughout the church, with ships' models and other memorabilia.

Sacred Heart Church

Omagh, Co Tyrone

This Roman Catholic church, dating from 1899, has two unequal spires, dominating this attractive market-town.

Drumlane Church

Milltown, Co Cavan

Drumlane Church and Round Tower were part of an Augustinian abbey foundation.

The siting of the monastery was inspired, as the fourteenth-century church and earlier tower are beautifully situated between Drumlane and Derrybrick lakes. An unusual feature of the Round Tower is the engraving of a cock on the north face, thought to symbolise the Resurrection. The present buildings occupy the site of a sixth-century monastery which was founded by St Mogue, a pupil of St David of Wales.

St Patrick's Church

Donegal, Co Donegal

This Roman Catholic Church designed by Ralph Byrne is situated in the east of the town. Known as the 'Church of the Four Masters', it was built in 1931. Architecturally, it is almost the last example of the Celtic Revival movement and incorporates the statutory Round Tower and a west doorway that is Neo-Romanesque with chevron decoration in the archrings.

Left: Sacred Heart Church, Omagh, Co Tyrone.

MUNSTER

St Finn Barre's Cathedral

Cork, Co Cork

A monastic settlement was founded on the River Lee in the seventh century by St Finn Barre, a native of Connacht, who it is believed died *c*.623. A cathedral was demolished in 1735, but we do not know the date of its construction (though it was thought to be mediaeval). In 1735 a second cathedral was built in a Classical style, and, always unpopular, was demolished in 1865. In the words of one critic: 'Architectural beauty was not aimed at, nor was it achieved.' Another one wrote of 'the deformity of its exterior.'

Work began on The Cathedral Church of St Finn Barre (Church of Ireland) in 1865, and though it was consecrated in 1870, its towers and spires were not completed until 1879. In the French Gothic style, its most startling feature is the fact that its height greatly exceeds its length, giving a sense of the building 'rising up' on approach. Designed by William Burges, its interior too is richly decorated, making it arguably the most beautiful cathedral of the Church of Ireland.

Ennis Cathedral

Ennis, Co Clare

Erected in 1831, The Pro-Cathedral of St Peter and St Paul (Roman Catholic) was designed by Dominic Madden of Galway. Its Neo-Gothic structure is comparatively modest and simple, since money was not as plentiful in this region as it might have been in Dublin or Belfast. Almost totally devoid of representational stained glass, the reredos is however particularly noteworthy with its paintings of the Ascension and the Saints Peter and Paul.

Left: St Finn Barre's Cathedral, Cork.

Killaloe Cathedral

Killaloe, Co Clare

The Cathedral Church of St Flannan (Church of Ireland) was founded about 1185 by Domhnall Mór O'Brien, a twelfth-century king of Munster. It is sited on an earlier Romanesque church – the doorway of which is preserved in the south-west corner of the cathedral. St Flannan, whose name survives in the dedication of the cathedral, is a shadowy figure whom we know very little about, though his feast day is 18 December. The cathedral is in the form of a cross, and has three narrow lancet windows in the east gable. Beside the Romanesque door near the main entrance is one of the few stones in the country with a Viking runic inscription. Like most buildings of its type it has been extended over the centuries: the height of the tower has been increased twice (most recently in 1892, to allow the hanging of a peal of bells), whilst the twelfth-century nave was repaired between 1708 and 1711. Standing on a bed in the Shannon, the cathedral has being generally well maintained, something that had caused it to win a number of admirers.

The Cathedral of St Mary and St Anne

Cork, Co Cork

Construction of The Cathedral Church of St Mary and St Anne (Roman Catholic) began in 1799, one of the earliest post-Reformation Roman Catholic cathedrals. The interior was rebuilt by George Richard Pain in 1828 following a fire, though much of his design has been lost following J.R. Boyd Barret's 1960s revamp. The tower dates from 1862. The fact that it was built at all was largely due to Canon Daniel Foley (d. 1875), who having decided the cathedral needed a tower, acted as clerk of works, director of operations, mason and labourer. Its uneven style has led some to speculate that the untrained Foley may also have been its architect.

Rosscarbery Cathedral

Rosscarbery, Co Cork

A monastic settlement was founded at Rosscarbery in the late sixth century by St Fachtna, who is said to have died *c.* 600 at the age of forty-six. We do not know exactly when The Cathedral Church of St Fachtna (Church of Ireland) was built, though a church which stood on its site was wrecked during the Rebellion of 1641. Records are incomplete, probably due to Rosscarbery's distance from Dublin. In 1582 the Bishop of Ross described the town as being 'in so desolate and barbarous a place as it is not fit for an Englishman.' Rebuilding took place in the late seventeenth century, when much of the mediaeval masonry must have been demolished. The round-headed arch standing in the churchyard is probably a relic of the mediaeval cathedral. Some parts survive in the present cathedral, and there is no pervading architectural style – the building incorporates, for example, both Georgian and Gothic windows.

Cloyne Cathedral

Cloyne, Co Cork

An early Christian monastery was founded here by St Colman Mac Lenen who died around 600, but all its buildings were burned in 1137. The Cathedral Church of St Colman (Church of Ireland) was started around 1250, but because of much modernisation, comparatively little of this early church can be seen. The building itself is somewhat weathered, and it has been described as looking 'aged and forlorn'.On the opposite side of the road is the Round Tower; its original conical top was later replaced by battlements after the tower was struck by lightning in 1749.

The Cathedral Church of St Colman

Cobh, Co Cork

St Colman's Cathedral (Roman Catholic), overlooking Cobh, carries within its walls the traditions of thirteen centuries of the Diocese of Cloyne. It is dedicated to St Colman who founded the diocese in

560AD. Colman was a poet bard to the court of Aodh Caomh, King of Munster, but he left palace life to become a priest. He founded his monastery at Cloyne, on the eastern shore of Cork harbour, traces of which still survive.

Designed by the architects Pugin and Ashlin in a Neo-Gothic style, work began on the cathedral in 1868. (Pugin was the son of A.W.N. Pugin, who designed the Catholic cathedrals at Enniscorthy and Killarney.) It took 47 years to build, and was finally completed in 1916 when its 42 bells were installed (though five more bells were added in 1958). The largest bell is 200 feet above the ground and weighs 3.5 tons. Home to a magnificent, 2,468-pipe organ, the cathedral is a regular venue for recitals. The interior of the building combines Gothic grandeur with delicacy and a sense of the past – intricate carvings evoke the history of the Church in Ireland from the time of St Patrick through to the twentieth century.

Christ Church Cathedral

Waterford, Co Waterford

Two churches in Waterford stand on the site of Viking foundations: St Olaf's and Christ Church. It's assumed that St Olaf's was founded in the ninth century, but was rebuilt first by the Normans and then again in the eighteenth century. The Cathedral Church of the Blessed Trinity (Church of Ireland), or Christ Church as it is commonly known, was probably founded in the eleventh century. If eighteenth-century paintings and engravings are anything to go by, the cathedral evolved over the years into a disparate collection of buildings. These were subsequently demolished, and work began on a new cathedral in 1774. Designed by John Roberts in a Classical style, one of the criticisms of the building has been that its decorative embellishments appear light next to the over-heavy mass of the tower. Most of the woodwork was lost in a fire in 1815, but even more of the original Georgian interior was lost following extensive reworking in the late nineteenth century. Architectural historians have lamented the loss of the curious mediaeval buildings in favour of what has been likened to 'a good large old parish church in a third-rate English town.'

Holy Trinity Cathedral

Waterford, Co Waterford

The Cathedral Church of the Holy Trinity (Roman Catholic), was, like its Waterford Church of Ireland counterpart, also designed by John Roberts. Roberts was over eighty when he drew up the plans, and would rise every day at 6am to supervise the proceedings. One morning he rose at 3am by mistake, waited about in the half-built cathedral, and caught a chill from which he died. It is somewhat ironic that the building has been described as 'warm, luscious and Mediterrenean'. Executed in a Classical style, Thackeray visited it early in the 1840s and called it 'a large dingy chapel, of some pretensions within; but, as usual, there has

been a failure for want of money.' A touch of luxury has appeared more recently however: eight large Waterford glass chandeliers were donated in 1979.

St John's Cathedral

Limerick, Co Limerick

The Cathedral Church of St John the Baptist (Roman Catholic) opened in 1864, though a church dedicated to St John in Limerick can be traced to mediaeval times. Built of local limestone in a Gothic style, ten years after completion of the tower and spire the building was already in need of major restoration. The interior of the building is simple, with white plaster walls and dark stone piers, and the elongated, replacement spire is said to be one of the most beautiful in Ireland.

St Mary's Cathedral

Limerick, Co Limerick

Inspired by the Cistercian monasteries, The Cathedral Church of St Mary (Church of

Ireland) was completed in 1194. There is no overriding single style, but includes both Romanesque and Gothic features (apparently the design was altered during construction). Only parts of the Romanesque west doorway, nave, aisle, and transepts survive. The earliest chancel was built by the first bishop, Donnchadh, who died in 1209, but the present chancel was built in the fifteenth century. Possibly the most unique feature of the cathedral is the black oak misericords (choir stalls) which were carved around 1489, the only example of their kind in Ireland. Their detailing is intricate, and displays a remarkable assortment of figures and animals. Visitors are permitted to climb to the belfry and view the bells, which date from 1678.

Church of Ireland Cathedral (Cashel Cathedral)

Cashel, Co Tipperary

The Cathedral Church of St John the Baptist and St Patrick's Rock (Church of Ireland) is a spartan, elegant construction. Built between 1749 and 1784), its clear, dignified exterior is at odds with the shambolic medley of styles to be found within. Many different bits and pieces have been added over the years, beginning with the removal of the Georgian pews in the nineteenth century, in favour of more overblown Gothic and even some Romanesque fancies.

Athassel Abbey

Tipperary, Co Tipperary

This ruined Augustinian priory is situated on the west bank of the River Suir. Established in 1192, Athassel is believed to have been the largest medieval priory in Ireland until it burned down in 1447. The scattered monastic site conveys a tranquil atmosphere, from the gatehouse and church to the remains of the cloister and chapter house. The church has a fine west doorway, nave and chancel walls, as well as a fifteenth-century central tower.

Misericords (detail), St Mary's Cathedral, Co Limerick.

Ardfert Cathedral, Co Kerry.

Ardfert Cathedral

Ardfert, Co Kerry

The Cathedral Church of St Brendan goes back to the twelfth century. Roofless, the cathedral is in ruins, though its walls are largely standing. Its oldest parts are the Romanesque doorway and blind arcade on the west wall, as well as some masonry under the two windows in the north wall. In the middle of the thirteenth century the nave-and-chancel church took its present shape, with its characteristic triple lancet window in the east wall and the nine slender windows in the south wall. The remains of a Franciscan friary stand to the east of the cathedral: two sides of the cloister and part of the refectory survive. The ruins of a Round Tower fell to the ground in 1771. An eye-witness thought it was 'near one hundred feet high'. There is no surviving trace.

Molana Abbey

Waterford, Co Waterford

This abbey, standing on the site of an island monastery founded in the sixth century by St Maelanfaidh, was re-founded for the Canons Regular of St Augustine towards the close of the twelfth century. The church is rectangular, and may contain elements from an older church; it is lighted by ten fine lancet windows. On the east side of the cloister is the Chapter Room, where Raymond Le Gros is said to have been buried in 1186, while there is a refectory on the south and a kitchen on the west side of the cloister. A two-storey building to the north of the choir of the church was probably the prior's lodging.

Ardmore Cathedral

Ardmore, Waterford

It is believed Saint Declan founded a monastery in Ardmore in the fifth century.

St Declan's Cathedral, Ardmore, Co Waterford.

Ardmore Cathedral (it enjoyed a brief existence as the seat of a bishop in the late twelfth and early thirteenth century) stands as a ruin – its many styles from various periods still visible. The oldest section is the chancel which dates from the ninth century. It ceased to be used as a parish-church in 1848, when a new one was built on the hill. There are no remains of any monastic building.

Killone Abbey

Clare, Co Clare

The remains of an Augustinian nunnery dedicated to St John, founded in 1180 by Donal Mór O'Brien, King of Thomond. The holy well of St John nearby was a place of pilgrimage. The nunnery lies in the grounds of Newhall House (designed by Francis Bindon in the eighteenth century), on the banks of Lake Killone.

Holycross Cistercian Abbey

Clonmel, Co Tipperary

One of the first relics of the True Cross to have reached Ireland was presented to this abbey in the twelfth century, hence giving it its name. The abbey was founded by the great church builder, Donal Mór O'Brien, and its relic made Holycross a much visited place of pilgrimage during the later Middle Ages. It was the pilgrims' generous offerings, no doubt, which enabled the abbey to rebuild the church.

The extensive rebuilding included a magnificent chancel and transepts with a beautiful east window and graceful ribbed vaulting. The tracery windows of the transept chapels are also of the highest quality, making this church perhaps one of the finest to be built in the fifteenth century.

Between the two east chapels of the south transept, is an uniquue structure with elaborate columns and arches known as 'The Monk's Walking Place'. It is thought that its once housed the relic.

Cahir Abbey

Cahir, Co Tipperary

The Abbey of Our Lady was founded in the thirteenth century in the reign of King John by Geoffrey de Carnville, a Norman Knight. It was an Augustinian foundation of the Order of the Canons Regular. It has a high central tower, which was converted into a dwelling house after the Reformation. Part of another tower remains. The outbuildings reached as far as the river. Cahir Abbey was in full use for over 400 years and is currently being restored.

Monasteranenagh Cistercian Abbey

Limerick, Co Limerick

This Cistercian abbey was founded by the king of Limerick, Turlough O'Brien, around 1150 and completed thirty years later. In 1579, Sir John of Desmond was defeated by Sir Nicholas

Malby, who fought for the English. Malby then turned his cannon on the Irish seeking refuge in the abbey, destroying the refectory and cloister, before putting everyone inside to death. Further damage was done to the site when the belfry and chancel collapsed in 1807 and 1874 respectively.

Killagha Augustinian Abbey

Ardfert, Co Kerry

The abbey was erected on the site of an older monastery of St Colman some time after 1216 and dedicated to Our Blessed Lady. Only the church, with a single long nave, is still standing today. The windows, doors and niches of sandstone date from the thirteenth century, while the limestone work, including the fine east window, was inserted in the fifteenth century. The abbey was suppressed in 1576 and the domestic buildings to the south were destroyed by Cromwell's soldiers.

Kilcooly Cistercian Abbey

Tipperary, Co Tipperary

A Cistercian abbey founded from Jerpoint by Donal Mór O'Brien in 1182 and dedicated to the Virgin Mary and St Benedict. The church, built around 1200, had a nave and two aisles, but after the almost complete destruction of the monastery in 1445, great reconstruction took place within the monastery and the church lost its two aisles. In the course of rebuilding, a new north transept and a tower were also added. Little or nothing remains of the domestic buildings, but a two-storey building standing not far from the church was probably an infirmary. In the field approaching the abbey there is one of the few remaining examples of an Irish columbarium (a dovecot).

The Rock of Cashel

Cashel, Co Tipperary

The Rock of Cashel, rising out of the surrounding plain, is the most dramatic of all Irish monuments. It first appears as a fortification of the Eoghanachta kings of Munster in the fourth century. It was allegedly visited by St Patrick who converted Aenghus, the king of the time. St Patrick stuck his crosier through the king's foot during the baptism by mistake, and the king bore it with fortitude thinking that it was part of the ceremony.

In 1169 Donal Mór O'Brien founded a cathedral, which was superseded in the thirteenth century by the present structure. The cathedral was apparently burned (but not extensively) in the late fifteenth century by Gerald FitzGerald, and when asked by Henry VII why he had done this, he explained that he did it because he thought that the archbishop was inside. After the Reformation, Elizabeth I appointed the Archbishops of Cashel, and the most notorious of these was Miler MacGrath who held three other bishoprics as well and who, after he had died at the age of a hundred, was buried in the cathedral. In 1647 Cashel was the scene of terrible fighting in the Confederate wars. The cathedral was already ruined by the eighteenth century.

The cathedral has a nave, chancel, two transepts, a tower at the crossing and a residential tower at the western end. The choir was built first, and was erected probably around 1230. The east windows have gone, but there are five lancet windows in the south wall. The south transept was probably added by Archbishop MacKelly who died in 1252, while the north transept, the crossing and the nave were probably built by Archbishop MacCarwill around 1260. The tower above the crossing was added in the fourteenth century. On the other side of the chancel of the cathedral is a Round Tower. It has been repaired recently after being struck by lightning.

Right: The Rock of Cashel, Co Tipperary.

St Dominic's Abbey

Near the Rock of Cashel, Co Tipperary

This was probably one of the first Dominican churches to be built in Ireland. it was founded by Archbishop David MacKelly whose seat was on the Rock immediately above the abbey. General chapters of the Dominican order in Ireland were held here in 1289 and 1307. Around 1480 Archbishop John Cantwell rebuilt the church after it had been accidentally burned. The church has a number of thirteenth-century lancet windows (some of them blocked up), and others were replaced by windows with flowing tracery in the fifteenth century. The cloisters have disappeared. A south wing was added to the church around 1270.

Hore Abbey

Near the Rock of Cashel, Co Tipperary

The Benedictines were settled here from Glastonbury by Philip de Worcester at the end of the twelfth century, but Archbishop David MacCarwill took it from them, and brought Cistercians from Mellifont to found a new Cistercian Abbey here in 1272. It was to be the last Cistercian foundation in Ireland before the Reformation. The Abbey was well endowed at first, but later became impoverished. It also had a leper house in the town of Cashel. Much of the church is thirteenth-century, and many of the masons employed in its construction also worked in building the cathedral on the Rock which dominates it.

Corcomroe Abbey

Burren, Co Clare

The abbey is supposed to have been founded by Donal Mór O'Brien in 1182, but it is more likely to have been built by his son Donal, who brought monks from Inishlounaght around 1195. The church is cross-shaped, with each transept having one chapel. The choir is constructed in stone, and decorated with plants – opium poppy seed and lily-of-the-valley – as well as human heads. A gate arch which existed outside the monastery fell in 1840.

Canon Island

Killadysert, Co Clare

Donal Mór O'Brien founded a church on this island in the Shannon estuary for the Augustinian Canons some time towards the end of the twelfth century. The present church is long and rectangular, and was built early in the thirteenth century. In the fifteenth century a tower was built and two chapels – one at the south-east corner, the other to the west of the tower – were added. The whole monastery was surrounded by an older circular wall. We know little of the island's history while the monks inhabited it except that Mahon O'Griffy, Bishop of Killaloe, was buried there in 1483.

Inichicronan

Tuamgraney, Co Clare

Standing on an earlier monastic site founded by St Cronan, the church was granted to the Augustinian Canons of Clare Abbey by Donal Mór O'Brien in 1189. Sited on a quiet peninsula, the church probably dates to this period. By 1302 it had become a parish church. In the fifteenth century conventual buildings were added, of which some parts remain.

Quin Abbey

Quin, Co Clare

Founded by the MacNamaras in the middle of the fourteenth century, the abbey incorporated some of the curtain wall of the Anglo-Norman castle (built around 1280 by Richard de Clare). The cloisters were erected in 1402 and remain one of the features of the abbey. The Franciscan friars came later in the century. The view from the top of the tower is spectacular.

Ennis Abbey

Ennis, Co Clare

Founded by the O'Brien family in 1250 for the Franciscan Order close to the River

IRISH CATHEDRALS, CHURCHES, AND ABBEYS

Fergus, this friary was restored about 1300 by Turlough Mor O'Brien, who added the strikingly tall east window with its five slender lights and pointed top. Its monuments are famous, notably the fifteenth-century McMahon tomb with its carvings of the Passion.

Mothel Abbey

Waterford, Co Waterford

The original monastery was founded in the sixth century by St Cuan or St Breoghan, but was re-founded for the Augustinians by the Power family, presumably in the thirteenth century. It was closely associated with St Catherine's Abbey in Waterford. After the Suppression of the Monasteries in 1537, it passed to the Powers, but they were dispossessed half a century later. A few mediaeval wall fragments remain, but the best surviving feature is a tomb by Roricus O'Comayn.

Glenstal Abbey

Glenstal, Co Tipperary

It was intended that the building, with its Windsor-style tower and Norman gate, would look like a twelfth-century castle. As well as building the castle, the Barringtons transformed the surrounding land into beautiful grounds, planting trees and shrubs and constructing a number of artificial lakes. In the 1920s the family decided to move to England and sold the castle and lands to the Benedictine Order. The first monks arrived there from Maredsous, Belgium, in 1926. In 1957 the Glenstal house was formally raised to the status of abbey.

Right: Ennis Friary, Ennis, Co Clare.

LEINSTER

St Patrick's Cathedral

Dublin, Co Dublin

Perhaps the best-known cathedral in Ireland, it is worth pointing out that, according to the correct definition of the word, The National Cathedral and Collegiate Church of St Patrick (Church of Ireland) is not actually a cathedral. It is only the bishop's 'cathedra' or throne which confers cathedral dignity on a church. And St Patrick's is not subject to the jurisdiction of any bishop.

The site of the cathedral was traditionally associated with St Patrick, and old stones preserved in the nave show evidence of an earlier church on the site. These date back to the time of the saint himself, who is said to have baptised converts in a well nearby. Excavations in 1901 found what was

Left: St Patrick's Cathedral, Dublin.

thought to have been the remains of a well, which it's believed may have flourished until the sixteenth century.

Unlike the elevated position of Christ Church, St Patrick's is built on marshy lowland – making the provision of a crypt impossible. In 1213 the church was raised to cathedral status, and was almost totally rebuilt in the years following. It was around this time that the Lady Chapel at the east end of the choir was built.

In 1316, the spire was blown down and the church was damaged by fire when the citizens burned the suburbs on the approach of Edward Bruce. After the fire, the north-western part of the nave and the four western bays of the north aisle were rebuilt by Archbishop Thomas Minot, who

Top Left: Interior of St Patrick's Cathedral; Far left: Plaque outside the Cathedral;
Left: Exterior view of the Cathedral.
Above: Bust of Jonathan Swift (1775), by Patrick Cunningham. Swift was author of 'Gulliver's
Travels' and served as dean to the Cathedral from 1713-1735. His death mask is in the
Cathedral, as is his grave.

also built the great tower at the western end of the north wall. The stone vault of the nave collapsed in 1544.

After the Reformation, the cathedral was reduced to the status of a parish-church. During the Cromwellian period, it was used for courts martial and the stabling of horses (but then this was no means unusual). The interior was virtually wrecked by the time of the Reformation. (An appeal to the citizens of Dublin in 1660 spoke of its 'decayed and ruinous state'.) Large portions of the present church are the result of rebuilding carried out by Sir Benjamin Guinness from 1864 onwards. The renovation was careful, keeping in mind original structures, so that even though the building looks much as it did in the thirteenth or fourteenth century, most of the stonework has in fact been replaced.

Since 1871, when St Patrick's became the National Cathedral of the Church of Ireland, it has been used extensively for national occasions.

St Mary's Pro-Cathedral

Dublin, Co Dublin

Nobody knows who designed the Pro-Cathedral of the Immaculate Conception of the Blessed Virgin Mary (Roman Catholic). The winning design was sent from Paris and was marked with the letter 'P'. The identity of the architect continues to provoke speculation and argument.

The Pro-Cathedral is a Classical Revival building, one of the last of its kind before the craze for Gothic set in. Had plans been drawn up even just five years later, a very different style of building might have emerged. That said, it was originally intended to be the most impressive Roman Catholic church in Ireland. Certainly, its noble Greek Doric portico is scholarly and correct, and the form of the building as

Right: St Mary's Pro-Cathedral, Dublin, Co Dublin.

a whole demonstrates a mastery of composition.

St Mary's is one of the finest Neo-Classical buildings in Ireland, and its influences are predominantly French exemplars. It is perhaps sited in a somewhat cramped position and some of the street furniture in the vicinity does not rise to the occasion.

Stained-glass window in St Mary's Pro-Cathedral, Dublin.

Christ Church Cathedral

Dublin, Co Dublin

It is believed that The Cathedral Church of the Holy Trinity (Church of Ireland) was founded around 1030 – probably around the time the previously pagan Vikings became Christian – on the site of an original Viking church. It was largely due to John Cumin, the first Anglo-Norman archbishop, that the Hiberno-Norse cathedral was replaced with the Romanesque and later Gothic cathedral, parts of which survive today.

The cathedral is an important part of the national heritage and a heritage of the Church of Ireland, and is considered to be of enormous architectural importance. In 1395 King Richard II sat in state in the cathedral to receive homage from the kings of the four Irish provinces. In 1487 Lambert Simnel, pretender to the English throne in the reign of Henry VII was 'crowned' in Christ Church as Edward VI.

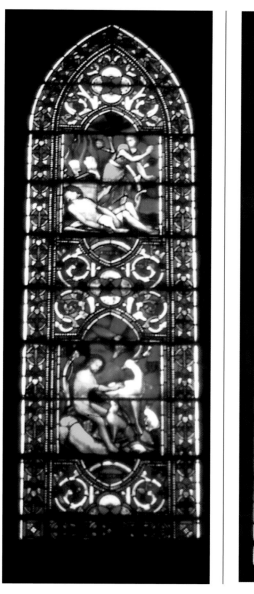

Stained-glass windows from the interior of Christ Church.

In 1689 King James attended Mass here and for a brief period, the rites of the pre-Reformation faith were restored. One year later, returning from the Battle of the Boyne on 6 July 1690, King William III gave thanks for his victory over King James II and presented a set of gold communion plate to the cathedral.

As well as providing a consistent site for worship over the last millennium, the building has had other uses. The crypt was used as a market during the sixteenth and seventeenth centuries, a meeting place for business, and at one stage even a pub (as a letter of 1633 shows). Even the vaults were converted into tippling houses for beer, wine and tobacco.

In 1742 the cathedral choir together with the choir of St Patrick's cathedral sang at the world premiere of Handel's Messiah in nearby Fishamble Street.

The cathedral as it exists today is heavily Victorianised due to the extensive restorations carried out by the architect George Edmund Street (between 1871-8). The renovations were paid for by a whisky distiller, the Dubliner Henry Roe, who donated £230,000, a vast sum in those days, to save the cathedral. More recently, a two-year restoration of the cathedral roof and stonework was undertaken in 1982, and in 1984, Kenneth Jones of Bray installed a new organ. Further work since 1997 has included the renewal of the heating and lighting systems and the restoration of the massive twelfth-century crypt.

Right: Christ Church Cathedral, Dublin.

St Stephen's Church, Dublin, Co Dublin.

St Stephen's Church

Dublin, Co Dublin

This lovely Anglican church is known as 'The Pepper Canister' on account of its distinctive dome. Designed by John Bowden and completed in 1824, it was one of the last churches built in the Georgian style by the Church of Ireland.

Its architecture is derived from three Athenian monuments: the Erechtheum (porch); the horologium of Andronicus (clocktower) and the monument of Lysicrates (campanile). It was extensively restored in 1992.

St Catherine's Church

Dublin, Co Dublin

A large rusticated building of 1769 by John Smyth with an imposing Roman Doric façade, this building bears the finest Georgian church front in Dublin. Its spire, like so many city churches, was never completed. In 1803, Robert Emmet, the United Irishman who led an unsuccessful attack on Dublin castle, was hanged on a scaffold erected outside the church, and his head then struck off. It was near here that his adherents had shortly before murdered Arthur Wolfe, Lord Chief Justice Kilwarden (1739-1803).

St Catherine's Church, Dublin.

St Mary's Abbey

Dublin, Co Dublin

Founded in 1139, St Mary's Abbey was the most prominent of the monasteries of the English Pale for four hundred years, from the twelfth century to its suppression in the middle of the sixteenth century. Originally founded as a daughter house of the Benedictine Order of Savigny, the abbey became Cistercian in 1147. Nothing survives of the original church apart from some floor tiles which were discovered in the nineteenth century. Only the chapter house and a passage to the south of it remain. Situated below street level, the chapter house is a vaulted room, largely used to house exhibitions.

St Michan's Parish Church

Dublin, Co Dublin

This Anglican church has a history dating back to Viking foundations in 1095. The present building is an early nineteenth-century restoration of a church built in 1685-86. Inside the church is a keyboard

Right: Newman's University Church, Dublin.

on which Handel played. In the vaults lie rebels brothers Henry and John Sheares (1778-1803 and 1766-78), respectively. Also in the vaults are several mummies of so-called 'crusaders' (probably seventeenth-century, which have been preserved by the moisture-absorbing magnesian limestone.

Newman's University Church

Dublin, Co Dublin

Adjoining a house is a miniature Byzantine-Romanesque basilica, decorated in the manner of an Italian church of the eleventh-century. Stylistically it is totally at variance with the Gothic or Classical tradition of nineteenth-century Irish church-building, and makes a fair claim to be one of remarkable church interiors in Ireland. It was created while John Hungerford Pollen in 1855, was Professor of Fine Art at the Catholic University. Entered through a brick porch which leads by a descending passageway from the street and through a forest of columns with variously carved capitals under the balcony, the

building opens out into a tall narrow painted rectangle. The church perfectly reflects Newman's ambition – to 'build a large barn and decorate it in the style of a basilica'.

St Audoen's Church

Dublin, Co Dublin

Dublin's only surviving mediaeval parish-church, of which the twelfth-century tower and west door and a fifteenth-century nave aisle remain intact. Beneath the tower is the tomb of Lord Portlester and his wife (1496), while the aisle contains a font of 1194 and some battered monuments of the Segrave family.

St Doulagh's Church

Dublin, Co Dublin

The church, dating back to the thirteenth-century, is the oldest church still in use. Externally its appearance is a complex arrangement of shapes. The church is a vaulted rectangle with an attic whose walls support a steeply pitched roof. The tower to the west end of the church contains a number of anchorites' cells built above a ground floor chamber, said to be the burial place of the hermit saint, St Doulagh.

St Mary's Chapel of Ease

Dublin, Co Dublin

This church, usually known as the 'Black Church', so named because it was built of black Dublin culp, stands on a plot presented by Lord Mountjoy. Built in *c*1830, many consider tthe church to be the best work of John Semple, often rated as one of the most interesting architects in the first half of the nineteenth-century. The interior is even more original than the exterior, and features an interesting vaulted ceiling. The church is deconsecrated and now used for commercial purposes.

St Audoen's Church Dublin, Co Dublin.

Kildare Cathedral

Kildare, Co Kildare

The Cathedral Church of St Brigid (Church of Ireland) has been destroyed and rebuilt more than most. It stands on the site of a church which was burned in the ninth century. Succeeding churches were also burned, until the first cathedral was built by Ralph of Bristol around 1223. In the rebellion of 1641, the cathedral was burned once more, though part of it was subsequently rebuilt. The remainder was constructed in 1875.

Kildare is where St Brigid is supposed to have founded her first convent. It is believed that the cathedral stands on the original site, but this is by no means certain. The Round Tower nearby is also of interest, largely due to the position of its doorway, fourteen feet from the ground. The church was comprehensively re-edified by GE Street in the nineteenth century.

St Canice's Cathedral

Kilkenny, Co Kilkenny

Completed in 1285, The Cathedral Church of St Canice (Church of Ireland) is the second largest mediaeval cathedral in Ireland. Though the original tower collapsed in 1332, it was replaced 20 years later. The condition of the building however went into decline, and though some refurbishment took place post-Reformation (this cathedral suffered particularly at the hands of Cromwell), it was not until 1864 that restoration was properly initiated. Today the cathedral appears remarkably well preserved. A Round Tower stands in its grounds, dated 700-1000AD.

Ferns Augustinian Abbey

Ferns, Co Wexford

This Augustinian abbey was founded by Dermot MacMurrough, probably on or near the site of the primitive oratory of St Mogue. The abbey was burned down in

Right: Interior of St Canice's Cathedral, Kilkenny, Co Kilkenny.

1154, but MacMurrough rebuilt it in 1160 and died there in 1171. The remains consist of a tower, the north wall of the church and the priests' residential apartments. The only remains of the cathedral are the ruined chancel and some fragments of the piers of a nave arcade, which are built into the walls of the modern building now used as a parish church and cathedral.

Dunbrody Cistercian Abbey

Wexford, Co Wexford

The abbey was founded for the Cistercians between 1175 and 1178 by Hervey de Montemarisco, uncle of Strongbow and Marshal of Henry II, and he became its first abbot. The ownership of the Abbey was much disputed during the early fourteenth century, but in 1342 it was finally decided that it belonged to St Mary's Abbey in Dublin, from where the original Cistercian monks had probably come. During the course of this dispute, Philip de Churchill, the abbot, was deposed

because of insubordination, and because he refused to submit to an inspection of his monastery by monks from St Mary's Abbey in Dublin. Edward III seized the Abbey and its possessions in 1348 because the monks refused to exercise hospitality or give alms.

Tintern Cistercian Abbey

Wexford, Co Wexford

During a stormy crossing to England, William, the Earl Marshall, made a vow that he would found a church in Ireland if he survived the voyage. He survived, and fulfilled his vow around 1200 by founding Tintern Abbey, named after its more famous counterpart in Wales (from where its first monks came). The church consisted of a nave and aisles, a chancel and transepts. The chancel was converted into living quarters after 1541, and several mullioned windows were inserted. The tower, which had been added to the church in the fifteenth century, was also converted into residential quarters. The nave and tower were occupied up to the twentieth century, but ongoing conservation work renders access difficult.

Selskar Abbey

Wexford, Co Wexford

Founded by the Roche family for the Canons Regular of St Augustine, the abbey was dedicated to Saints Peter and Paul in the thirteenth century. The surviving parts of the nave are fifteenth-century, the tower dates from the fourteenth century. Henry II is reputed to have done penance here for the murder of Thomas à Becket. The ruins are very attractive and there are some interesting old graveslabs in the grounds.

Baltinglass Cistercian Abbey

Baltinglass, Co Wicklow

In 1148 Dermot Mac Murrough brought Cistercian monks here from Mellifont to found a new monastery which he called 'The Valley of Salvation', and Baltinglass in turn was the mother-house of a number of other Cistercian foundations including Jerpoint, County Kilkenny. The monastery was the centre of a number of disputes in the thirteenth century, one with the Archbishop of Dublin and another in which the monks were accused of harbouring 'felons against the English'. The church consisted of a nave with aisles, chancel and two transepts, and building was probably complete by 1170. Joining the south aisle to the cloister is a twelfth-century doorway, while excavations in 1931 brought to light a north door in the aisle, parts of the original cloister (now rebuilt) and an early tower which blocked the eastern two-thirds of the transept arches. The decorative stonework at Baltinglass shows an interesting fusion of Cistercian and Irish Romanesque architecture.

Overleaf: Tintern Abbey, Co Wexford.

Above: Nun's Church, Clonmacnois, Co Offaly.
Overleaf: St Kevin's Kitchen, Co Wicklow.

St Kevin's Church

Glendalough, Co Wicklow

Known as 'St Kevin's Kitchen' and consisting of a church, cell and watchtower, this is the most interesting and best-preserved of the church-remains at Glendalough, an ecclesiastical seventh-century site ascribed to St Kevin. The church is a fine example of a two-storied oratory with a steeply pitched stone roof.

Bective Abbey

Bective, Co Meath

Bective Abbey was founded in 1150 by Murchadh O'Melaghin, king of Meath, for the Cistercians, and was dedicated to the Blessed Virgin. It was an abbey of some importance as the Abbot was a spiritual lord and sat in the Parliament of the Pale. The abbey was suppressed in 1536 and the lands were rented to Thomas Asgarde, and eventually bought by Andrew Wyse in 1552. It passed into the hands of the Dillons and then the Boltons, before falling into ruin. The cloister is the best preserved of the buildings and there is a pillar of a figure carrying a crozier. There are also some beautiful arches which are still intact.

Clonmacnois

Co Offaly

This is among the most important early Christian monastic sites in the country. It was founded by St Ciaran around 545-548. The site includes the ruins of a cathedral, eight churches (including the Romanesque Nun's church *c*1166 with its decorative doorway and chancel arch), two round towers, three high crosses and a large collection of Christian grave slabs.

Abbeyshrule Cistercian Abbey

Abbeyshrule, Co Longford

A Cistercian abbey was founded in Abbeyshrule in 1150 – one of the earliest in the country. The abbey was founded by the O'Farrells and was eventually closed by Elizabeth I during the Tudor suppression of the monasteries. The adjoining graveyard contains part of the only high cross in County Longford.

Abbeylaragh Cistercian Abbey

Abbeylaragh, Co Longford

A Cistercian abbey founded by Richard Tuit in 1211 and colonised from St Mary's in Dublin in 1214. It was pillaged by Edward Bruce in 1315. The only surviving parts of the abbey are the crossing of 1214,

Mellifont Abbey, Trim, Co Meath.

and the tower inserted over it in the fifteenth century. A semi-circular earthwork north of the village is regarded locally as the site of the original church founded here by St Patrick about 460.

Mellifont Cistercian Abbey

Louth, Co Louth

St Malachy of Armagh brought a handful of monks with him from Clairvaux and founded the first Irish Cistercian monastery here in 1142. St Bernard of Clairvaux sent a skilful architect named Robert to help build the church, and this is reflected in the rounded chapels in the transepts. The monastery was burned early in the fourteenth century. Comparatively little of the church remains, but one feature discovered during excavations was a crypt under the porch at the western end of the church. Its most spectacular survival is the octagonal two-storey lavabo in the middle of the south side where there was originally a fountain in which the monks washed their hands before going in to eat in the refectory nearby. By the first half of the thirteenth century the monks had become lax, and there were many irregularities, including insubordination, both in Mellifont and in its daughter houses. In 1223 the pope intervened, and in 1228 Stephen went so far as to ask the abbot of Clairvaux to move the monastery to another site in order to rid the monastery of the dissension.

Aghaboe

Aghaboe, Co Laois

The site of St Canice's Monastery in the sixth century, Aghaboe was plundered in 913, rebuilt in 1052, burnt in 1116, rebuilt in 1234, and again burnt in 1346. The nineteenth-century church on the site of the Augustinian Priory church retains thirteenth-century pieces from the Dominican abbey.

Graiguenamanagh Duiske Cistercian Abbey

Graiguenamanagh, Co Kilkenny

William the Marshall founded an abbey here for the Cistercians in 1207, though the monks may have settled here before that date. They stayed here for more than three centuries, until the abbey was dissolved by Henry VIII. One of the best-preserved Cistercian abbeys in Ireland, its church was splendidly restored in the 1970s. Although earlier restorations of 1813 and 1886 have covered much of the walls, the decoration of the capitals and the shapes of the arches can still be seen. It is one of the few mediaeval churches in Ireland in which Mass is still celebrated.

Old Abbey

Drogheda, Co Louth

Shortly after the Norman invasion, about 1206, a hospital for the sick and infirm was founded here by Ursus de Swemele and his wife. Care of the hospital was given to a religious community. By the end of the thirteenth century, it was taken over by the Augustinians or Crutched Friars, and the subsequent history of the abbey was an uneventful one. At the Dissolution, the abbey was surrendered in 1543 by the last prior, Richard Malone. The Corporation subsequently disposed of the monastic property by leases, which accounts for the amount of commercial building in the Abbey precincts. All that remains of this once extensive abbey is the central belfry tower, and a piece of gable wall to the west.

Fore

Mullingar, Co Westmeath

Fore has the most extensive Benedictine remains in Ireland. It is the site of the ruins of St Fechin's Monastery, and was a Benedictine Priory until 1539 when it was suppressed by Henry VIII. The present building belongs in the main to the fifteenth century. There are nine ancient crosses within a radius of a mile from the village. Near the foot of Ben Fore is

a large moat, reputed to be an early Anglo-Norman fortification. There are also some slight remains of the walls and gateways which surrounded the mediaeval town.

Fore Abbey

Delvin, Co Westmeath

An early Christian monastery was founded here around 630 by St Fechin, who died of the plague in 664-5. At one time there were 300 monks in the monastery. It was burned in 771, 830 and again in 870, and a number of times in the course of the eleventh and twelfth centuries. From this old monastery one church – St. Feichin's – survives, standing in a graveyard above the road. This was built early in the thirteenth century; it has three round-headed east windows, but the north wall is largely a modern reconstruction. The eastern and western sides of the domestic buildings around the cloister have been much modified, and portions of the fifteenth-century cloister were re-erected in 1912.

Jerpoint Abbey

Thomastown, Co Kilkenny

One of the finest Cistercian monastic ruins in Ireland, it is believed the abbey may have been founded in 1158 for the Benedictines, by Donal Mac Gillapatrick, king of Ossory. The eastern end of the church may date to as early as 1160, though the original east window was replaced by the present window in the fourteenth century. The rest of the church was built about 1180, and although the aisles have bluntly pointed Gothic arches, the capitals are still Romanesque in character, as are also the round-headed windows in the west wall. The cloister (which has been excellently restored to some of its former glory), dates from the fifteenth century and displays a fascinating variety of figure sculpture, including saints and knights.

Right: Jerpoint Abbey, Co Kilkenny.

CONNACHT

The Cathedral of the Assumption

Tuam, Co Galway

When the site was initially obtained in 1830, it was rented for a shilling a year. The original architect was Dominic Madden, (who also designed Ennis Cathedral), though he left the project in 1839 after being told he had to make the chancel smaller. Constructed in limestone in a Decorated Gothic style, The Cathedral Church of the Assumption of the Blessed Virgin (Roman Catholic) has a striking, three-storey tower. The six turrets terminate in eight octagonal spirelets, which Thomas Carlyle described as 'like pots with many ladles.'

Kylemore Abbey,

Connemara, Co Galway

This unique Abbey is the only home of the Benedictine Nuns. Built originally as a Castle in 1868 for Mitchell Henry, the son of a wealthy Manchester merchant, it is one of the best examples of Irish Neo-Gothic architecture.

Clonfert Cathedral

Clonfert, Co Galway

The original monastery was founded here by St Brendan in 563 and it is here that this great saint is buried. The earliest part of the present Cathedral Church of St Brendan (Church of Ireland) dates to the twelfth century. Its doorway is the crowning achievement of Irish Romanesque decoration. It is in six orders, and has an amazing variety of motifs. Heads abound – both human and animal – and more human heads appear in a pointed hood above the door. The early thirteenth-century east windows in the chancel can be numbered

Left: Kylemore Abbey, Connemara, Co Galway.

among the best late Romanesque windows. The chancel arch was inserted in the fifteenth century, and is decorated with angels, a rosette and a mermaid carrying a mirror. The supporting arches of the tower at the west end of the church are also decorated with fifteenth-century heads, and the innermost order of the Romanesque doorway was also inserted at this time. The sacristy is also fifteenth-century. The church had a Romanesque south transept which is now in ruins.

Galway Cathedral

Galway, Co Galway

The Cathedral Church of Our Lady Assumed into Heaven, and Saint Nicholas (Roman Catholic), dominates Galway's skyline. Built on the site of the old Galway Gaol, the foundation stone was laid on 27 October 1957. Constructed from rough-hewn, greenish-grey limestone, the design has a slightly Iberian feel, recalling Galway's mediaeval trading links with Spain. Other than that, its architectural style

generally defies classification: its round arches and unplastered stonework evoke Romanesque architecture, at odds with the Renaissance cupolas on the towers. The cathedral was dedicated in August 1965.

Kilmacduagh Cathedral

Galway, Co Galway

The Cathedral Church of St Colman dates largely from the fourteenth and fifteenth century, though earlier parts survive. Other additions include Tudor windows and some seventeenth- and eighteenth-century tombs. Dotted around the site is one of the finest collections of churches in Ireland. Best known is the excellently preserved Round Tower, which shares a lean (38.3cm to the south-west) with its more famous counterpart at Pisa. This tower however, built of the local limestone – is twice as old. Beside the tower is the cathedral, of which the west gable, with its blocked-up, flat-headed doorway (dating from the eleventh or twelfth century), is the earliest part. In a field to the north, is St

Loughrea Cathedral, Co Galway.

John's Church, a small church with rounded and pointed windows which probably dates from the twelfth century. To the north-west is O'Heyne's Church, built in the first half of the thirteenth century with a beautiful chancel arch supported by piers with animal and floral decoration. East of the cathedral, and on the other side of the road, is St Mary's – a church with a round-headed east window, built around 1200. All of these churches were heavily plundered early in the thirteenth century. Moss-covered mounds are all that remain of the Church of St Colman.

Loughrea Cathedral

Loughrea, Galway

The Cathedral Church of St Brendan (Roman Catholic) is a comparatively small building, set in grounds which slope gently down towards a lake. Completed in 1902, it has been described as 'a tasteful piece of modern Gothic'. Designed by William Byrne, the exterior of the cathedral might appear unpromising, but the interior is crammed with Celtic Revival carving, metalwork, and textiles of the highest order. The building of the cathedral coincided with a major renaissance of Irish arts and crafts, and this is reflected in the richness of the decoration which can be found within the building. The glazing is particular spectacular.

St Mary's Cathedral

Tuam, Co Galway

Searching for an idea or inspiration about where to establish his monastery, St Jarlath was told by St Brendan of Clonfert to drive his chariot until his wheel broke. The wheel broke at Tuam. Founded in the late fifth or early sixth century (St Jarlath is said to have died *c.* 550), in the late twelfth century a Romanesque nave-and-chancel church was built. The nave collapsed in 1184, and

Left: Detail of Clonfert Cathedral, Co Galway.

was presumably rebuilt, though when it was completed, and how long it survived is unclear. The Cathedral Church of Saint Mary (Church of Ireland) was entirely rebuilt in the nineteenth century, though in the aisle of the south nave the shaft of a twelfth-century High Cross has been retained, with interlacing and other ornament.

Knock Shrine

Knock, Co Mayo

Knock is the scene of the apparition of the Blessed Virgin Mary, St Joseph, and St John on 21 August 1879, and was witnessed by fifteen local people. Since then, it has been a place of devotion and pilgrimage. Numerous miracles also have been recorded over the years. On 30 September 1979, His Holiness Pope John Paul II visited the shrine, as part of his pilgrimage to Ireland. The focal point of the shrine is the gable of the apparition, on the west wall of the Church of St John the Baptist, and the Shrine Oratory. The beautifully landscaped site has hostels for the sick, two rest houses for invalids, as well as a chapel of reconciliation.

The Cathedral Church of St Mary the Virgin and St John the Baptist

Sligo, Co Sligo

The Cathedral Church of St Mary the Virgin and St John the Baptist (Church of Ireland). The architect was the German-born Richard Cassel, who also designed Leinster House in Dublin. The cathedral was substantially altered in the nineteenth century, with the addition of battlements, so that the building now resembles a small castle. Cassel's original interior was marked by a large central chamber where the congregation would gather, but this was reworked when the craze for Gothic set in. The building has ended up being a hotch-potch of architectural styles, though the overriding impression remains somewhat plain and parochial.

Cathedral of the Immaculate Conception

Sligo, Co Sligo

The Cathedral Church of the Immaculate Conception of the Blessed Virgin Mary (Roman Catholic) is lofty and impressive, built 1869-74 in a Romanesque Revival style. Consecrated in 1874 by Cardinal Cullen, Archbishop of Dublin, it was designed by George Goldie of London and executed in cut limestone. Extensively renovated in 1975, most of the original furnishings have been retained, including the high altar. A separate, new altar contains a relic from a recently canonised saint, St Oliver Plunkett (1975).

The Abbey of St John

Lecarrow, Co Roscommon

The Abbey of St John, (named after St John the Baptist), was endowed in the days of St Patrick. It passed into the ownership of a Mr Hudson, who called it the Manor of St John and which today gives us the name Hodson Bay. The annual feast day was June 25 and, for years, large numbers would gather there to celebrate. But, as time went on, dealers from Athlone availed themselves of the opportunity to set up a market where everything from flax yarns, apples and gingerbread, were for sale. Dancing and skirmishes of all sorts interfered with those who came to say their prayers, and occasional fighting put an end to the wayward festivities. The earlier tradition had been revived in recent years and is celebrated in a more congenial atmosphere.

Boyle Cistercian Abbey

Boyle, Co Roscommon

One of the best preserved in Ireland, this Cistercian abbey was colonised from Mellifont in 1161. The building of the chancel, and the transepts with their side-chapels, must have begun shortly after this date, though the lancet windows in the east gable were inserted in the thirteenth century. The large, square tower formed part of the church from the beginning,

though it was raised in height at a later stage. The five eastern arches of the nave and their supporting piers were built at the end of the twelfth century, and have well-preserved capitals typical of the period. Nothing remains of the cloister, but on the eastern side there are two doorways of *c.* 1200, now blocked up, while on the west side there is a two-storey gatehouse. The abbey was one of the most important in Connacht, and in 1659, it was occupied by the Cromwellians who carried out a great deal of destruction.

Sligo Abbey

Abbey Street, Co Sligo

The abbey was founded around 1252 for the Dominicans by Maurice Fitzgerald, Second Baron of Offaly, who was also founder of the town. Having escaped

Boyle Cistercian Abbey, Co Roscommon.

the ravages suffered by the now destroyed Sligo Castle in the thirteenth and fourteenth centuries, the friary was accidentally burned in 1414, but was rebuilt two years later. The choir, with its eight lancet windows, is the oldest part of the church and dates to shortly after the foundation. The sacristy and the chapter house beside the cloister are both thirteenth-century buildings, but the cloister itself and the other buildings around it were built in the fifteenth century. Note the window in the north wall of the first floor where the reader in the refectory had his desk.

Murrisk Abbey

Westport, Co Mayo

In 1457 the Augustinian, Father Hugh O'Malley, was granted permission to build a church and priory in Murrisk, at the foot of Croagh Patrick. The Augustians were forced to leave their sanctuary in 1577 and it now in ruins. The east window behind the

Right: Sligo Abbey, Co Sligo.

146

Carving at Sligo Abbey, Co Sligo.

altar is the finest architectural feature which remains. It has five trefoil pointed lights surmounted by interconnecting bar tracery and according to Dr H. Leask, the Irish authority on church building, is arguably 'the best window of its type in the west of Ireland'. The ruins of Murrisk abbey have been declared a national monument.

Ballintubber Abbey

Claremorris, Co Mayo

Ballintubber Abbey was founded in 1216 by Cathal Crobhdearg O'Connor, king of Connacht, near the site of the church built by St Patrick in 441. Despite the abbey's turbulent history, which includes burning, the building now has the unique status of being Ireland's only royal abbey which has been in continuous use for over 780 years.

Cong Abbey

Cong, Co Mayo

Situated on the site of an earlier monastery founded in the seventh century, this is an Augustinian abbey which is thought to date from the twelfth century, now in the grounds of Ashford Castle. It probably replaces a church which was burnt in 1137. Of the church itself comparatively little remains, and the fine Romanesque doorway was inserted into the north wall in modern times. This doorway contains some very fine sculpture. Like most of the rest of the building, it probably dates to around 1200, (though the church was possibly built slightly later). The best feature is the cloister which was also erected in the 1220s but has been reconstructed. The decorated stonework is exquisitely executed, and is probably the finest work of its type in the west of Ireland.

Inishmaine Augustinian Abbey

Inishmaine, Co Mayo

The church was built, perhaps for a nunnery, in the early part of the thirteenth century, and consists of a nave and chancel. The church is entered through a flat-headed doorway in the north wall which may have been taken from an earlier church on the same site and inserted here, or could be one of the latest uses of this type of doorway in Ireland. Not far away from the church is a gatehouse, probably of fifteenth-century date, which gave access to the monastic enclosure. The monastery was burned in 1227 by High, son of Roderic O'Connor, but it probably continued to exist for a long time after that.

Errew Abbey

Mayo, Co Mayo

Errew Abbey was founded by the Barretts for the Augustinian Canons in 1413. The church is a long rectangular building. Although much of the dressed stonework has fallen, there are some good trefoil windows remaining. The ground floor of the domestic buildings is preserved on the eastern wing of the cloister, but otherwise little of these buildings remain.

Moyne Abbey

Ballina, Co Mayo

Moyne Abbey and Rosserk Abbey are located close to each other, north of Ballina. Both compete for the title of largest and most impressive ecclesiastical ruins in Mayo.

Moyne was founded by the Burke family as a Franciscan friary. Built in the late Irish Gothic Style, it was consecrated in 1462. This abbey was destroyed in the 1590s by Queen Elizabeth's governor of Connacht, Sir Richard Bingham.

Ballintubber Augustinian Abbey

Ballintubber, Co Mayo

In 1216 Cathal O'Conor, King of Connacht, founded a monastery here for the Augustinians on the site of an older monastery, and some parts of the church date from this time. In 1465, charges were investigated against the abbot for waste and improper use of the properties and revenues of the abbey, but we do not know what the outcome was. The monastery was dissolved in 1542, and it was subsequently leased to various private individuals. In 1635 the Augustinians petitioned to the Pope for permission to take over the abbey once again, and they seem to have regained possession as a result. The church was partially restored in 1846 and in 1889, but the final restoration was carried out from 1963 and was finished in time for the 750th anniversary of the foundation in 1966. The abbey is unusual in being able to boast that Mass has continued to be celebrated throughout the 750 years of its existence.

Fenagh Abbey

Ballinamore, Co Leitrim

About three kilometres from Ballinamore lies a ruined mediaeval church built on the site of an early Christian monastery. The abbey was used for a time as a place of Church of Ireland worship until the present church was built around 1798.

Athenry Abbey

Athenry, Co Galway

This was founded in 1241 by Meiler de Bermingham. Accidentally burned in 1423, it was rebuilt with a central tower and the present northern doorway. Restored in 1638-44, it was declared a university for the Dominican Order by decree of a General Chapter held in Rome. In 1652 it was totally wrecked by the Cromwellians – like so many others.

Knockmoy Cistercian Abbey

Knockmoy, Co Galway

An abbey dedicated to the Blessed Virgin Mary, and founded for the Cistercians from Boyle in 1189-90. The church has a nave, chancel and a transept with two chapels. The nave is simple and austere, with little ornament except at the top of the piers. In contrast, the rib-vaulted chancel has beautifully carved stonework with fine capitals and east windows. In 1240 the abbot was censured for having his hair washed by a woman.

St Nicolas of Myra

Galway, Co Galway

St Nicolas of Myra is the largest mediaeval parish church in Ireland still in constant use. It was built on the site of an earlier chapel. Christopher Columbus prayed here in 1477 when he visited Galway. The church also contains many beautifully carved tombs, including the tomb of James Lynch, the first mayor of Galway, who condemned his own son to death for murder and then personally hanged him.

Picture Credits

Irish Tourist Board: 18, 84, 91, 104, 121, 124, 126, 128, 139, 140
Northern Irish Tourist Board: 11, 14, 25, 31, 58, 61, 62, 69, 70, 73, 74, 82
Heritage Images: 6, 21, 92, 94, 99, 103, 118, 130, 135, 136, 145, 147, 148
Joe Tracey of McCormick Tracey Mullarkey: 54, 55, 57

Further Reading

C E B BRETT (1967): *Buildings of Belfast 1700-1914* (London: Weidenfeld & Nicolson)
_____ (1996): *Buildings of County Antrim* (with photographs by MICHAEL O'CONNELL)
    (Belfast: Ulster Architectural Heritage Society and the Ulster Foundation)
_____ (1999) *Buildings of County Armagh* (with photographs by MICHAEL O'CONNELL)
    (Belfast: Ulster Architectural Heritage Society)
CHRISTINE CASEY and ALISTAIR ROWAN (1993): *North Leinster* in *The Buildings of Ireland* series
    (London: Penguin Group)
MAURICE CRAIG (1982): *The Architecture of Ireland from earliest times to 1880*
    (London: B T Batsford Ltd, and Dublin: Eason & Son Ltd)
JAMES STEVENS CURL (1986): *The Londonderry Plantation 1609-1914: The History, Architecture, and*
    Planning of the Estates of the City of London and its Livery Companies in Ulster
    (Chichester: Phillimore & Co Ltd)
_____ (2000): *The Honourable The Irish Society and the Plantation of Ulster,1608-2000. The*
    City of of London and the Colonisation of County Londonderry in the Province of Ulster
    in Ireland. A History and Critique
    (Chichester: Phillimore & Co Ltd)
DESMOND GUINNESS (1979): *Georgian Dublin*
    (London: B T Batsford Ltd)
PAUL LARMOUR (1987): *Belfast: An Illustrated Architectural Guide*
    (Belfast: Friar's Bush Press)
_____ (1992): *The Arts and Crafts Movement in Ireland*
    (Belfast: Friar's Bush Press)
GEORGE PETRIE (1845): *The Ecclesiastical Architecture of Ireland, anterior to the Anglo-Norman Invasion;*
    comprising an essay on the Origin and Uses of the Round Towers of Ireland
    (Dublin: Hodges & Smith)
AUGUSTUS WELBY NORTHMORE PUGIN (1843): *Contrasts: or, A Parallel between Noble Edifices of the*
    Middle Ages, and Corresponding Buildings of the Present day; shewing the Present day Decay of Taste
    (London: Charles Dolman)
_____ (1843): *An Apology for the Revival of Christian Architecture in England* (London: John Weale)
_____ (1853) *The True Principles of Christian Architecture;*
    set forth in Two Lectures delivered at St Marie's, Oscott
    (London: Henry G Bohn)
ALISTAIR ROWAN (1979): *North West Ulster* in *The Buildings of Ireland* series
    (Harmondsworth: Penguin Books)
JEANNE SHEEHY (1977): *J J McCarthy and the Gothic Revival in Ireland*
    (Belfast: Ulster Architectural Heritage Society)
SIMON WALKER (2000): *Historic Ulster Churches*
    (Belfast: The Institute of Irish Studies, The Queen's University of Belfast)

Readers are also referred to the substantial publications of the Ulster Architectural Heritage Society, many of which deal with individual districts and their buildings. The Irish Georgian Society is also responsible for several admirable publications to be consulted with profit.